To my family and friends, treasures beyond all else—
Compassionate hearts, keepers of the past, storytellers
and charmers who fill the present moment with love
and laughter and ride life as a great adventure.

WOODLEAF LEGACY

The Story of a California Gold Rush Town

WOODLEAF LEGACY

The Story of a California Gold Rush Town

By Rosemarie Mossinger

with an Introduction by DeWitt Whistler Jayne,
Professor Emeritus, Humanities

CARL MAUTZ PUBLISHING
1995

DESIGNED BY RICHARD D. MOORE
AND ROSEMARIE MOSSINGER.
EDITED BY JEANNE CHAPMAN.
COMPOSED IN ADOBE GARAMOND AND MERIDIAN.
PRINTED AND BOUND IN THE U.S.A.

FRONT COVER: WOODLEAF HOTEL,
COURTESY FLORENCE PRATER;
BLACK BART, COURTESY WELLS FARGO BANK.
FRONTISPIECE: WOODLEAF STORE,
COURTESY AGNES FALCK.

First Edition
1 3 5 7 9 10 8 6 4 2

HARDCOVER ISBN 0-9621940-2-6
SOFTCOVER ISBN 0-9621940-4-2
LIBRARY OF CONGRESS CATALOG NO. 94-077982

CARL MAUTZ PUBLISHING
228 COMMERCIAL STREET, SUITE 522
NEVADA CITY, CALIFORNIA 95959
TELEPHONE: (916) 478-1610
E MAIL: FOLKIMAGE@AOL.COM

Contents

Acknowledgments

MANY PEOPLE AND INSTITUTIONS were of great help in locating files, documents and photographs, and provided information and clues for further research. I appreciate the kind assistance of the staff of the Bancroft Library, California State Archives, California State Law Library, California State Library, California State University Chico Meriam Library Special Collections, De Young Museum, Huntington Library, Indiana University Lilly Library, Mooretown Rancheria Library, National Archives, Plumas County Museum, Plumas National Forest, Smithsonian Institution, Sutter County Superintendent of Schools Educational Resource Center, Wells Fargo Archives, Young Life Woodleaf, Yuba and Butte County Archives, Yuba County Library, Yuba Feather Historical Association; and Mary Ellen Bailey, Linda Brennan, Robert Cermack, Helen Falck Dunning, Jack Dunning, Agnes Riker Falck, Ben Falck, Charles Falck, Lawrence Falck, Lorraine Mullins Frazier, Henry French, Jann Garvis, Jay Grimstead, John Hendrickson, Kathe Goria-Hendrickson, Dorothy J. Hill, Bill Holmes, Marge Holmes, Bob Jacoby, Chuck James, William A. Jones, David Knox, Jim Lague, Lona Lahore, Robert Mackensen, Edwin Magruder, Philip McDonald, Sandra Dunning Noel, Wes Owen, Bill Prater, Mary Ellen Reynolds, Pam Bush, Lloyd Silva, Zelma Wood Skoog, Dennis Woll and Steve Woods.

I am grateful to Jim Lague and Ben Falck for their painstaking work with old prints, negatives and glass plates. Many photographs were made available for this edition of *Woodleaf Legacy* only because of their skill and generosity.

The arrival last year of a box of photographs and documents was a wonderful surprise. To the sender who continues to remain anonymous, thank you.

Thanks to friends, family and associates who read the various drafts of the manuscript through the years, offering suggestions and pointing out errors: E. F. Muster, Marge Holmes, William Ingersoll, De Witt Jayne, Dennis Woll, Jon and Christina Mossinger, Sally and Gary Plount, Jill and Steve Bathauer, Bill Taylor, Jani Blakemore, and Winston Culp. The text has been greatly improved because of their insight. Thanks to my husband, Don, who seldom complained as the binders and files filled the shelves, but rather, built more shelves.

The book's design is the work of Richard D. Moore and the editing of the text was done by Jeanne Chapman, both skilled professionals who graciously led me through the process. Carl Mautz's steadfast enthusiasm and friendship has at last brought the project to completion, producing the book you are holding. May it bring you pleasure.

Introduction

EARLY IN MARCH OF 1966 a friend invited me to accompany him from Sacramento to the recently vacated lumber town of Woodleaf, which the Young Life organization had purchased for conversion into a summer camp for high school young people. It was a miserably cold, dismal, rainy day and the snow in the woods was a foot deep and melting. My interest was in determining if there was anything of historic or antique value to be salvaged from the place.

The town itself was quite small, beautifully situated among the evergreen trees, and was all of post World War II vintage—not exactly old. All that could be seen from the road was a deserted roadside restaurant and the old "Woodville House" hotel, which was over a hundred years old and distinctly showing its age. This building was entirely empty except for a small cubicle in one corner that still served as a U.S. Post Office. No antiques were to be seen at all—and then it slowly dawned on me that there was *the* antique, the building itself! Fortunately the new owners of the town agreed. They decided to save and restore it for use as headquarters for the new camp.

At this point Rosemarie Mossinger entered the picture. Young Life is an international organization with headquarters in Colorado which owns camping properties in the United States and Canada. Each camp has its own resident management team, and Don Mossinger, Rosemarie's husband, joined the staff and moved the family to Woodleaf. Rosemarie, a native of Northern California, lived in Woodleaf for a few years as a child and had many friends in the area, and she became the unofficial public relations person for the Young Life Camp. She had previously developed a keen interest in local history, interviewed many old-timers and did exhaustive research in old newspapers as well as in state, county and court records. In time she was asked to write the official historical monograph for the centennial celebration of Yuba County, and she led the campaign to have the old hotel officially listed in the National Register of Historic Buildings.

Many research experts manage to write up their findings in a style that is nearly as dry and uninteresting as the material that they are studying, but Rosemarie has the unique ability to get to the heart of her investigation in very human terms and then to express it in a most engaging and readable style. The author has included in this book an excellent selection of old wood engravings, photographs, maps, and her own pen-and-ink drawings.

This volume gives us a beautiful insight into the sparsely inhabited wooded outback in the detente period between the wars in the late nineteenth century. It seems light years away from the old Wild West of General Custer and John Wayne. On the other hand, upon occasion, there *were* those all-night dinners and dances at the old hotel that are almost beyond our twentieth-century comprehension. The history of the later years serves as a reflection, immediate and personal, of the changing world of our century, which has outgrown the need for even a rather elegant old stage coach hotel.

—DeWitt Whistler Jayne
Professor Emeritus in Humanities
California State University, Sacramento

Preface

WOODLEAF'S PLACE in the world is infinitely small—scarcely a speck upon the globe. But if we could peer through a magnifying lens and adjust the focus to the past, we would see a world in miniature, teeming with life, changing as the years swiftly pass. First, the dark-haired people moving among the trees, stalking deer and gathering acorns. Then, swarms of men of many colors and languages scurry everywhere, digging endlessly. Caravans of wagons and mule teams arrive, bringing women and children. Men run about with saws, trees fall, and in a frenzy of hauling and hammering, mills, hotels, shops and homes appear. Highways wind through the hills and dams are built across the rivers and streams. Families in trucks piled with tents and boats rush to the lakes. It is a dizzying progression, and we must pull back to see these people clearly. A few are famous, but most of them are ordinary folk doing familiar things. They buy groceries, suffer toothaches, go to work, fall in love, and stay up all night when their children are sick. They are like people anywhere in the world—they are like us. Their dreams, adventures, failures and joys are woven into the pattern of everyday living at Woodleaf, and it is the drama of their lives that captivates us.

There are only about six short paragraphs and a few scattered references about Woodleaf in the earliest histories. I began collecting stories and fragments of material starting in 1946, when I was eight years old and my family moved to Woodleaf. The swimming pool and tennis courts of the 1920s resort era were gone and the meadow had grown wild again. The enormous freight barn stood near the main road, the Coffin House was nearby, and the Woodleaf Store sold everything from fresh meat and vegetables to boots, linoleum, rope and penny candy. Our nearest neighbor was a distant relative of the Woodville tollkeeper, who lived there from 1873 to around 1906; the Falcks still lived in their family home. A few people remembered the Maidu people who once lived at Woodleaf, the huge cattle drives, the celebrations and the calamities, and shared with us their priceless photographs and diaries. The Falcks invited us to their home one evening. When it grew dark, Mr. Falck lit the flame in his "Magic Lantern," slid the glass plates into place, and images appeared of men logging with great teams of oxen, and of people lining the veranda of the hotel and preparing for a grand ball.

After ten years, I left for college and eventually moved to the Bay Area in California and married. Many years later, my husband Don was approached by the staff of the non-profit Christian organization, Young Life, and invited to join the staff and move to Woodleaf with his family. He accepted the offer, and we moved there in February of 1968. We were introduced to an exuberant group of people, and with them, we plunged into work and adventures that centered upon the gospel of Christ. We had the opportunity to be a part of Woodleaf's metamorphosis from an empty town to a place thronging again with people from every part of the world. Working side by side with friends who gave so much of their lives and talents; sharing sweat, aching muscles and lots of fun and laughter; singing and tearful goodbyes—all these are etched forever on our hearts.

During our ten years there, Don continued his

practice of recording events in a daily journal, and I kept a duplicate file of the town's history for Young Life. After we left in 1978, however, Woodleaf's history files and collection of original photographs and documents from the 1800s were taken to the dump.

In the past twelve years, my family and friends have helped find copies of some of the missing photographs and documents, and the Young Life staff at Woodleaf gathered material again. I continued to research every conceivable source for more information, but at times I grew weary of the whole project and packed everything away. Invariably, then, someone told me about another treasure, or I discovered the existence of diaries and letters in a library or private collection somewhere, and I was drawn back to it. At one point, a friend gave me the opportunity to read hundreds of documents, many of them unopened for 135 years, some full of surprises about Woodleaf's past.

Given the enormous amount of material, the challenge was to write an interesting story rather than compile a "Woodleaf Encyclopedia" of two thousand pages. Through the years, I had drawn up a chronology of all events and details of Woodleaf, and added to it as each fragment was found. I added a parallel chronology of depressions, wars, inventions, and natural disasters that might affect the town. A third parallel charted the lives of the people involved with Woodleaf. Every rumor and legend was included until I could either verify or discard it. Sometimes the truth was so startling that rumor could never match it for drama, as in the murders of 1852, the 1857-59 battle for Woodville, and the F.B.I. raid in the 1930s. By weaving upon the three parallel threads, the story slowly took shape, and was edited and trimmed into its present form.

History, though, is never finished. While a new page is added today, there are gaps remaining in the past that tease us, and questions without answers. Life sprawls in tangles of detail, and one cannot tie it into neat bundles without killing its essence. But there is always a possibility of finding another diary, photograph or document that will add to our knowledge of Woodleaf, and enhance our view of events and people. These treasures help us appreci-

ate the men and women who lived in times that were filled with labor, disease and conditions we naively think romantic, yet who preserved the intimate details of their lives, their world, as their legacy to us. This book, then, is our legacy to those who follow.

—Rosemarie Mossinger

Author's Note

WOODLEAF IS A SMALL TOWN with a rich heritage, located in the Sierra Nevada Mountains of California. It has been called many names: Barker Ranch, Abbott House, Woodville and Woodleaf. For millennia, however, it was known by still another name: Pakan'yani. The ancient land of the Maidu and the traditions of ten thousand years were overrun by fur traders and mingled with the dreams of pioneers searching for new homes. Add to this story the age-old tale of the greed for gold, and a remarkable saga unfolds. From the pages of diaries, letters, handwritten deeds and photographs, we can glimpse moments in the lives of those who have walked these hills and called them home.

Maidu boy with a red-shafted flicker feather headband and ornaments.
Photograph by A. W. Chase, c. 1871–1872. Courtesy Smithsonian Institution.

Chapter One
THE MAIDU
1760

Then it was Earthmaker, Earthmaker who spoke in ancient times, bringing this world into being.
—KAJNAHU

THE VILLAGE AT THE EDGE of the woods caught the first rays of the sun and people began to stir. Several women at the spring filled their baskets with water and carried them down to their fires, getting ready to prepare the morning meal. They chatted while pounding acorns into flour with stone pestles and mortars. From behind the bark houses a group of children chased each other onto the grassy slope, laughing and calling. Below the meadow in a tangle of vines, youngsters gathered berries. There were only a few older men in the village, working bone tools against stone, flaking off chip after chip to shape arrow points. An old dog stretched, then walked slowly toward the warmth of the fire. Some of the men had taken the young dogs out hunting; others had gone to a nearby village to invite their neighbors to a celebration and perhaps trade for shell jewelry or grain.

This moment from the past at Pakan'yani—"the marsh by the mountain"—is pieced together from Maidu descriptions of their life.[1] Some scholars believe the Maidu came here between ten thousand and forty thousand years ago, across the land bridge from Asia and down the western edge of the continent, but in the tradition of the Maidu they have lived here from the beginning of creation.[2] At times around 130 people lived in this village.[3]

Pakan'yani was one of several villages that belonged to a small nation within the Maidu tribe, each nation having its own leaders, customs and legends.[4] Even the language was a distinct dialect developed over many centuries.

From Pakan'yani, trails led in every direction to other villages. People traveled steadily between

them, trading goods, news and gossip, and giving and receiving invitations to village dances and special events.

The Maidu traded with other tribes for goods that were not available locally—obsidian for arrow points from the Achomawi to the north; grain and shells that served as money from the Wintun in the valley, and wild tobacco and other goods from the Paiute and Washo to the east. In return, the Maidu provided deer skins, antlers, venison and bows, which were especially prized by the valley tribes. The Maidu were excellent bowmen and made their bows of yew wood, which grows in the steep ravines on both sides of the pass dividing the Feather and Yuba rivers. Shell money was traded from tribe to tribe, reaching almost every group in California.[5] The shells were strung onto fine threads of sinew, and the women wore the necklaces on special occasions.

Contact with other tribes was not always peaceful. Raids by neighboring tribes were terrifying, and people were killed or captured to become the slaves or wives of their enemies.[6] The men attacked their enemies in retaliation, taking prisoners and hanging their scalps on poles, then dancing around the poles to celebrate their victory.

At the base of one slope was the *kum*, a sacred place of worship where ceremonies, dances and special gatherings were held. It was usually the home of the tribal leader or chief. The *kum* at Pakan'yani measured about thirty feet across, but in some villages they were as large as forty feet.[7] A circular area was dug to a depth of about two feet and a foundation of large stones laid around the perimeter. Log posts were erected around the edge, and poles

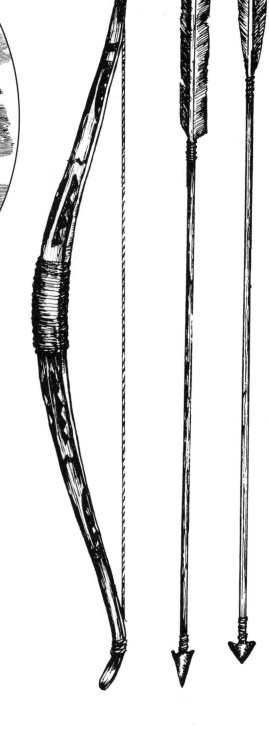

spanned the circle. These were lashed together with ropes made of rawhide. The exterior was finished with bark, and the inner walls were lined with woven mats. The homes of the villagers were made in the same manner, but were smaller in size.

The Maidu are a deeply religious people, and look upon the bounty of the land as a gift. They believe that neither men nor tribes own the earth, but are given use of it by the Great Spirit and must care for it in return. Earthmaker, or Wonomi,[8] formed the earth, and then created human beings of different colors to populate the world and to provide himself with companionship. This creation story was told by Kajnahu:[9]

Then it was Earthmaker, Earthmaker who spoke in ancient times, bringing this world into being. Laying down these mountains, these many great mountains, stone mountains, he went along in olden times in heaven, putting down into place the waters of the earth, moving over the country. Thereupon he said, "Let this be, this did I, Earthmaker, create long ago."

Top left: *The stone blade of a knife was fastened to a wooden handle with sinew.*
Top center: *Spearing salmon; by Charles C. Nahl.*
Right: *Dècorated bow; arrows with flint points.*

The country was a garden from which the Maidu gathered wild plums, berries, grains, nutmeg and a variety of nuts and root vegetables. Acorns and pine nuts were important staples of their diet. Great herds of elk and antelope roamed the hills and valleys. Salmon came up the streams to spawn in the fall; trout and freshwater mussels could be found throughout the year.

As in every garden, however, there were years when the fruit withered, the grain was skimpy and the oaks bore few acorns. Sometimes the hunters came back empty-handed, and the salmon were scarce. Dried meat, fruit and vegetables spoiled during unusually long rainy seasons; violent storms or hungry animals destroyed the granaries. The Maidu in one village might trade with other villages for food, unless their neighbors had experienced difficulties as well. The people knew lean times and suffering within the cycles of the natural world.[10]

Before the hunt, the Maidu held elaborate dance ceremonies, singing and praying for success. Prayers of thanksgiving were offered both to the Creator and to the animals who were asked to give their lives for the people.

Every summer the Maidu went east into the high Sierra for a month or more, taking along their dogs.

These small fawn-colored animals with short, pointed ears were well-treated pets, but were also working dogs trained to hunt.[11] The men went out day after day, bringing back venison and other game. Bear, elk or cougar were sometimes hunted, but only with a group of men who would tire the animal before the arrows were shot. Men stationed themselves at many points along a chase route, and as the animal approached, each man ran out in turn to take the place of his exhausted predecessor, leading the animal to the next point. This went on until the animal collapsed, or all the arrows were spent, or the animal outlasted the number of runners on the route. Boys learned to shoot and hunt while very young, and went out together after rabbits and birds.

The women stripped the meat, smoking or drying it over frames and filling the large food baskets for the winter. The furs were quickly treated and packed, to be made into cloaks, blankets, hats and bow quivers later in the village. Sinews from the deer strengthened the backs of bows and were separated into fine threads for sewing and stringing beads. Bones and horn were made into hide scrapers, awls and other tools. The brains were used to tan the hides. Nothing was wasted, since all life was a gift from the Great Spirit, and thus held sacred.

Left: *A Maidu woman gathering acorns; the basket is carried by a band around the forehead; by Charles C. Nahl.*
Right: *Basket with quail plume design. Photograph by Chris L. Moser, courtesy Riverside Municipal Museum.*

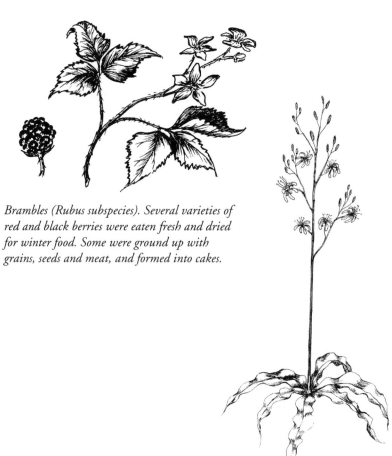

Brambles (Rubus subspecies). Several varieties of red and black berries were eaten fresh and dried for winter food. Some were ground up with grains, seeds and meat, and formed into cakes.

Bracken fern (Pteridium aquilinum). New fronds were eaten raw or cooked; roots provided colored strands for designs in baskets.

Soaproot (Chlorogalium pomeridianum). The bulb made suds for washing; when roasted, it formed a strong glue used to fasten feathers to arrow shafts. A thin solution brought relief from poison oak rash. When mashed and scattered in a stream, it stunned the fish temporarily and brought them to the surface, where they were gathered by the Maidu.

Wild plum (Prunus subspecies). Eaten fresh and sun-dried for winter.

Tan oak (Lithocarpus densiflorus). Not a true oak, but bears acorns that were gathered, shelled, dried, and ground into flour, an important staple of the Maidu diet.

In the fall, they made trips to Pomingo (Strawberry Valley) to gather plants, acorns, pine nuts and fruit for food and medicine. In the oak groves, children clambered among the tree branches, shaking the acorns down while others filled the baskets. Another trek was made to the river when the salmon were running. These camping trips brought together many hundreds of people, who looked forward to the good times of hunting, working and swapping stories while the children ran about, shouting and playing. A game similar to football was played, and there were foot races, dice games and shooting matches.

Back in Pakan'yani, the Maidu stored the food in granaries suspended on poles to keep out rodents and insects. The acorns were ground into flour using stone mortars and pestles. The hill above the present-day pond has many bedrock outcroppings among the oak trees where the Maidu fashioned their mortars, and from there the women of Pakan'yani could look out over the meadow as they worked, watching their young children and keeping an eye out for their returning menfolk.[12]

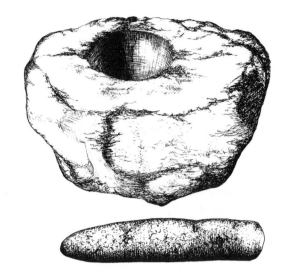

We used the seeds of a variety of grasses, including timothy and wild oats. Seeds from other plants such as lupine and mule-ears were also used, as were roots of many kinds. Those roots that were most principal to the diet included camas and wild carrot (Queen Anne's lace) . . . . Our people were constantly aware of the need for conservation. In gathering roots some plants were left for seed and the disturbed ground was always leveled off. Earth was mother, who furnished the food, and we were considerate not to leave her scarred. A few berries were left on bushes for birds and squirrels and other animals, not only for their own sakes, but because they too were future food for the people.
—Chankutpan[13]

This careful consideration of the earth and all things on it is a common attitude among Native Americans. The circle is a symbol of their knowledge that all of creation is connected.

Top: *Stone mortar and pestle used to make flour.*
Bottom: *Cradleboard, or ty-ty (pronounced tuh-tuh) with detachable sunhood. Photograph by Chris L. Moser, courtesy Riverside Municipal Museum.*

Fire was a part of the circle, and served many purposes besides cooking and heating. Many ceremonies took place around a fire and wooden tools were hardened over coals. For those suffering from pain or sickness, beds were made of boughs and leaves spread over warm ashes. The Indians took refuge from the hordes of voracious mosquitoes by sitting in the thick smoke of a campfire. The Maidu word corresponding to "July" is *kaui'tson,* which means "ground burn," and in the late summer each group burned off selected portions of its area. The fires kept the brush from becoming dense, and destroyed tree seedlings that would otherwise invade meadows. At the same time it added nutrients to the soil, which fostered the growth of grasses that the Maidu found desirable. The cycles of burning were controlled to produce the necessary results. Some plants were burned every two years, since only the two-year-old shoots of this plant were suitable for basket-weaving. Fields were burned every year, and the lush, tender grasses brought deer, rabbits and birds, and insured good hunting.

The men gathered and stored the supplies they would need for making new tools and weapons during the long winter days—yew wood for bows, wild mock orange for arrow shafts, horn for tools, obsidian for arrowheads. Leather was tanned and prepared for winding the shafts and fashioning snares for small animals and birds.

Before the cold weather began, each family repaired its home with thick slabs of cedar or pine bark, the cracks chinked tightly with moss.[14] The

Maidu hubo, *a temporary summer shelter made of bark on a pole frame. Courtesy Carl Mautz.*

inside was made comfortable and snug with fresh boughs on willow bed frames and rabbit fur blankets. Tools, bows, quivers of arrows and personal belongings were hung against the walls, and in the center of the room was the fire pit and cooking tools. The floor was packed clay—a surface as hard and shiny as tile.

I remember as a child living in the cedar bark house with my grandparents. How wonderful it was, lying awake at night sometimes, to hear the coyotes bark, and the hoot owls uttering their calls among the trees. Sometimes there would be the running clatter of squirrels on the bark slabs above us; and in the spring and summer, just as it grew light before the sun rose, there came the enchantment of the bird chorus, the orchestra of the Great Spirit all around us.
—Chankutpan

Baskets were used in almost every aspect of food gathering and preparation, but they were more than utensils. Maidu women developed basket-making into a distinct art form. The colors and textures of many kinds of plants were woven into intricate designs and shapes of great beauty. Some types were so tightly woven that they were used for cooking, not by being placed over the fire, but by holding a liquid mixture into which hot stones were repeatedly dropped. Girls learned to make the baskets by using leftover scraps and watching the women work. By the time they were eight or nine years old, they were gathering their own materials, curing them, and weaving designs into fine baskets.

The Maidu played several different types of musical instruments to accompany their singing. Clappers, whistles, musical bows, foot drums and rattles were used in ceremonies and for amusement. Flutes made of elderwood were played only for pleasure and courtship.

Marriages were sometimes arranged between two young people, but they were often the free choice of both man and woman. It was common for a young man to go to a neighboring village for a wife, since he was probably related to most of the people in his own village. He courted a young

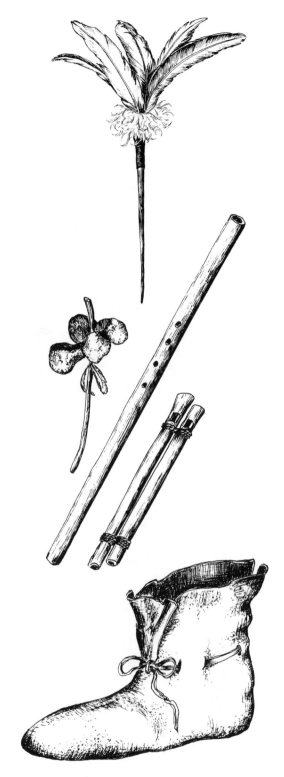

Top: *The Plume stick, decorated with feathers and down, was worn in a hat or carried in dances.*
Center: *Cocoon rattle, elderwood flute and whistles of bird bone.*
Bottom: *Moccasins were worn only during the winter, stuffed with soft grass for warmth.*

Top: *People from neighboring tribes and villages arrive at a Maidu village for a burning ceremony; by Tarbell and T. Hill.*
Left: *Figure of a man used in a burning ceremony; bobcat fur body, flicker feather headband, neck and head of otter fur, feather plume headdress, feather plume stick in right hand, basket of acorn meal in left hand.*

girl with gifts, music of the elderwood flute and conversation. If she accepted the gifts, after a time they were considered married.

The Maidu believed that the spirit of a dead person could do great harm if offended or if his or her name was spoken. Tribal and family history took the form of stories and legends relating events and experiences, but because names were often not mentioned, many of them were lost. During cremation, the person's heart or soul was released, traveling east until it joined the Great Spirit and all the Maidu ancestors in a place far beyond the earth. The ashes were buried in a place apart from the village, and were held in respect by the people.

A separate event called a "burning" was usually held in September or October to honor those of the tribal family who had died. During the year preceding the event, many things of value and beauty were made by the relatives—deerskin coats, elaborate feather capes, hats, lynx ornaments, beaded garments and baskets. These were placed on tall poles around the gathering area. After many friends from neighboring groups had arrived, a great fire was built, the singing and chanting began, and when the signal was given, the family took down the beautiful things from the poles and flung them into the fire. There followed a great feast prepared by the host families.

Storytelling was a popular pastime, especially in the long winter evenings. While snow fell outside and the fire burned low, the children fell asleep beneath their warm fur blankets, listening to the stories of Coyote, the legends of heroes and the songs of myth and worship. The stories told of their people living in harmony with all creation, following the pattern of the seasons measured by the moon and the stars, year after year for thousands of years.

Interior of a Maidu dwelling. At Left: a man repairs a fishing net; a woman and child rest on the upper bunk. Center: a woman grinds with mortar and pestle while a woman cooks. At right: an infant in a cradleboard, large gathering baskets, and duck decoys made of tule; by J. R. Bartlett.

Seth Kinman, trapper, 1865. Photograph by Matthew Brady. Courtesy Carl Mautz.

Chapter Two
THE FUR TRADERS
1767-1847

A country inhabited by a great many Indians …
I found beaver, elk, deer and antelope in abundance.
—JEDEDIAH S. SMITH, 1827

IN 1767, FAR TO THE SOUTH of Pakan'yani, in the lower portion of Alta California, the Spanish began to establish Franciscan missions to secure their claims to the territory. The areas to the north were scarcely affected, and there was little change for the Maidu except for the appearance of highly-prized European glass beads, which filtered northward in trade. At that time the entire people are believed to have numbered about 9,000.[1]

Spanish explorers began to push into the northern areas—Gabriel Moraga in 1808 and Luis Arguello in 1820. Arguello reached the juncture of two rivers, one of which he named for the great number of wildfowl feathers floating on it—El Rio de Las Plumas—the Feather River. The other river, the Yuba, was later named after the tribe living where it joined the Feather. The life of the valley Maidu began to change, but those in the hills were left alone for the most part, as the Spanish explorers did not venture far from the river valleys. Mexico's independence from Spain in 1822 brought Alta California under Mexican rule, but still the Maidu were far away from its influence.

The people of Pakan'yani followed the cycles of days and seasons as they had for thousands of years. In 1827 a baby was born to Ya'lo and his wife. In time, she was given a name by her parents or by the elders in the tribe. In Maidu tradition, a person's name was never used in his presence. Each person had a nickname that was used in speaking to him. Even a husband could not call his wife by her name, and to do so could be grounds for divorce. There was no reluctance for someone to say a person's name when out of their hearing, however, and so it

was learned that the child's name was Tasu'mili.[2]

The same year an American trapper, Captain Jedediah Smith, came up the Sacramento and Feather rivers and made contact with the Maidu and other tribes.[3] When he reached Fort Vancouver in 1828, he reported that the California streams were full of lynx, sable, beaver and otter; grizzly bears and great herds of elk, antelope and deer roamed the land, along with wild cattle and horses that had escaped from the Spanish ranchos. The Hudson's Bay Company quickly organized expeditions for California to harvest the furs before other American trappers arrived.[4] Both groups were encroaching on Mexican territory, and very few bothered to apply for Mexican passports and licenses, intent only on the fortune to be made in furs.

The tall beaver hats were all the rage in Europe, and gentlemen had at least one for every occasion. Ladies were wearing dresses and capes trimmed in otter and sable. The abundant elk, antelope and

The beaver's soft undercoat was made into felt for hats, and at the peak of the fashion, the hat industry used 100,000 pelts a year. News of the great numbers of animals set off a boom in trapping expeditions into the western wilderness.

wild cattle would provide plenty of meat for food, and skins for clothing and moccasins. Unlike the American trappers who traveled alone or with a few others, the Hudson's Bay brigades were composed of many trappers, hunters, their wives and children.

John Work's expedition for the Hudson's Bay Company left Fort Vancouver on August 17, 1832:

At the head of the brigade rode the leader, a chief trapper of the company, astride a strong limbed Nez Perce horse and armed to the teeth . . . He wore a bright red, knitted toque, and was clad in deerskin. A long rifle hung at his side, with his bright-beaded tobacco pouch and long knife. Directly behind him rode his Indian wife, gaily attired in the finest London broadcloth, with a wide-brimmed, feather-trimmed hat atop her wealth of long, shining, black hair. The bells on her leather leggings made a musical note as her pony jogged along.
—H. E. Bolton

John Work was forty years old and devoted to his Indian wife, Josette, half Nez Perce Indian, and half French, described as a woman of great beauty, outstanding character and dignity. She had a position of honor as the wife of the leader. On this expedition, their three small daughters were with them. Jane, nine months old, rode in a basket woven by Josette and hung from her saddle; the other two girls, Sarah, three, and Letitia, nearly five years old, rode close by on their own ponies.

Behind the lead group rode the trappers with their wives and children, followed by more than two hundred horses carrying trade goods and supplies. The brigade of over four hundred horses and mules stretched out along the trail for nearly a mile. John Work wrote in his journal:

My party [consists of] twenty-eight men, twenty-two women, forty-four children and six Indians, in all one hundred; Michel's [Laframboise'] party [of] eighteen men, twelve women, sixteen children, seventeen Indians, in all sixty-three, total one hundred and sixty-three persons.[5]

No proper European or American gentleman appeared in public without a beaver hat, and fur trimmed their capes and collars as well.

Breakfast at Sunrise. "With a Bowie you separate a large rib from the mass before you, hold firmly to the smaller end, and your outrageous appetite teaches all the rest," wrote Alfred Jacob Miller in 1832, when he traveled with the trappers and recorded their lifestyle on canvas. Courtesy Walters Art Gallery.

Laframboise was well liked, and was mentioned frequently in letters, mission records and diaries of other traders and trappers. While John Work and some of the others had one wife, Laframboise had many. "He says he has a wife of high rank of every tribe, by which means he has secured his safety," wrote Captain Charles Wilkes, a U.S. explorer in 1841.[6]

The trip from Fort Vancouver would cover thousands of miles, along the wild rivers of the Siskiyou, Cascade, Sierra and Coast mountain ranges, through the valleys of Oregon and California, as far south as French Camp (San Joaquin River), before the brigade returned to Fort Vancouver late the next year.[7]

They camped each night, setting up leather tents while the hunters went out for elk, bear and deer for the company's food, and set out traps for beaver. The men ranged far into the surrounding mountains and valleys for days at a time, exploring most of the territory of the Maidu and other tribes. Back at the main camp, they were divided into groups, and four trappers and their families shared a common fire. Pierre Legace, Work's father-in-law, was affectionately known as "Old Trapper," part of the group that gathered at the leader's campfire. The women dressed the skins of the animals, tanned the deerskins and made garments and moccasins for sale and trade, dried the meat, cooked the meals, washed and mended clothes, and tended the children.

Their expedition faced great difficulties from the beginning. After only a few days out, Joseph Larocque's wife, Marianne of the Cayuse, "remained behind in the sulks yesterday, he went back for her and brought her up today." Then, within weeks of starting from the fort, ten men fell ill with a mysterious fever, uncontrollable shaking and terrible pain; numbers of women and children soon followed. Work noted, "Though I was well supplied with medicines at Vancouver . . . it will soon be all done." Malaria had spread throughout California and Oregon, and the deadly illness dogged their steps for the entire journey.[8] On December 7, Work noted that the territory assigned to him had been hunted out, and no beaver were left. Another expedition's hunt "amounts to 950 beaver, which is far short of the number expected . . . so that the account given of this quarter was greatly exaggerated." Other trappers and hunters had heard the rumors of the abundant game and crossed each other's trails frequently. The party moved south into California during almost continuous rain, and vast areas of the valleys were flooded, the rivers high and dangerous.

Thursday, January 3, 1833. Frost in the morning, fine weather during the day. Moved a few miles farther down the river, to near where the low ground is all under the water. We cannot cross it here now, and even could we, it would be imprudent to risk with the camp when with a night or two's heavy rain we might lose all our horses and perhaps ourselves. There are several

villages of Indians near our camp. We must now return up the river and proceed along the high land towards the mountains.

Sunday, January 6. Raised camp and proceeded up the river to the fork and then up the E. fork 10 miles N. and encamped on a dry plain not far from the mountains. The greater part of the way soft and miry and pools of water all along a short distance from the river. The hunters out and killed 19 elk. Some of the men were also out with their traps 8 beaver were taken. I am anxious for the safety of [Laframboise'] party, as the people say where he was encamped the ground is low [near Wheatland].

Tuesday, January 8. Heavy rain in the night and greater part of the day. Did not raise camp on account of the bad weather. The people visited their traps and some who slept out returned. 10 beaver taken.

Wednesday, January 9. Raised camp and proceeded 10 miles S. E. This was a severe day's journey both on the people and horses . . . it was after dark before the people all arrived. The ground is so soft that the horses were wading up to the belly . . . through mud and water.

Thursday, January 10. Laframboise is coming on this evening to join us, they experience much difficulty on account of the high water which had pent them in on a small spot where they . . . could not stir and starving at the same time as there were no animals to be found. The Americans had crossed and were obliged to come

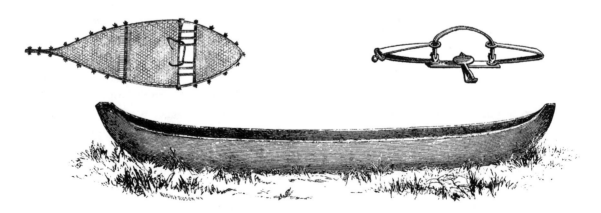

Snowshoe, beaver trap and canoe.

Trappers in a Snowstorm; by H. P. Sharp.

back again and are also coming this way. Under these circumstances we must also turn back where we may find some elk to subsist on.

Friday, January 11. The people out hunting but without success. In the evenings two Americans arrived starving, they left their party three days ago and had eat nothing since. We furnished them with food and lodging.[9]

Wednesday, January 16. The people out and set some traps, 4 beaver taken. In the evening M. Laframboise arrived with his party. Another of his men, Turner, has left him and gone to the Americans but he paid his debt and delivered up his traps and horses before he went off.

Friday, January 18. Fine weather. Raised camp, proceeded 15 miles S. W. to main fork of Feather river which we crossed. The hunters were out but with little success [north of Marysville].

Saturday, January 19. Heavy rain in the night and the greater part of the day. Did not move camp. The people started to hunt but the bad weather turned them back.

Sunday, January 20. Did not raise camp. The people out hunting and killed some deer, but it is nothing among many people.

Monday, January 21. Some rain, forenoon. Had got under way to move camp when it was found that 26 horses were missing, they had crossed the river in the night and when they were found it was too late to raise camp. Two are not yet found.

Wednesday, January 23. Fine weather. All hands out hunting and the women in the camp busily employed drying meat and dressing the skins. 81 elk, 10 deer and 1 bear killed [in the past few days]. The animals are mostly very lean [near the Buttes].[10]

Friday, January 25. Cloudy, fine weather. Gave orders to all hands to collect and prepare skins to make canoes when we have to cross rivers too deep to ford.

Thursday, February 7. A great many Indians came to the Butte . . . and were running the elk afoot.

The trade rate was generally seven beaver pelts for a blanket, three for a yard of wool cloth, and one for a copper pot. The prized Hawken rifle cost thirteen pelts. Below: A tin of tea from Hudson's Bay Company.

Thursday, February 21. Fine weather. The people out hunting but with little success. 3 elk and 8 deer killed. Some Indians visited us and got a little meat from the people.

Sunday, February 24. Fine weather. Continued our journey 15 miles N. N. W. up the river to near the mountains. L. Pichette had two traps stolen by the Indians . . . they are very numerous here. In about 1 1/2 hours march after we started this morning we passed four villages with 40 to 50 houses in each and there is another large village a little way ahead of us. They are seen out in the plains when overflowed, with nets set for wildfowl, they have stuffed skins of geese as decoys [near Oroville].

Later in the summer, the group encountered other difficulties. Swarms of "Muscuitoes" covered the valley, nearly driving them mad. "They are like to devour us," wrote Work. "All hands passed another sleepless night with the Musquitoes, they allow us no respite." One trapper, Michelle Oteotanin, was mauled by a bear, "a good deal torn in the arm and the back." He lingered in agony for nine days before dying, leaving a wife and two children. "Animals are becoming very scarce," wrote Work, noting that the continuous hunting was making them wary and shy of humans. Only a few months earlier, on February 22, he had written, "395 elk, 148 deer, 17 bears and 8 antelope have been killed in a month." Then Larocque's wife, Marianne, ran off with a Spaniard. "Since she left him he has been like a fool and not knowing what to do with himself . . . he ate and slept very little." Within a week, Larocque found her and brought her back, but three weeks later she was gone again, and this time, Pierre Satakaras' wife went with her. "The two men who went off on the 8th to seek after their wives returned with them," wrote Work. Larocque and Marianne apparently made up, for they stayed together during the rest of the trip.

The brigade's contact with some of the Indians was stormy, in spite of Laframboise' marriages, but their contact with the Maidu seems to have been peaceful. They met at several points along the rivers in the valley and at the villages in the mountains,

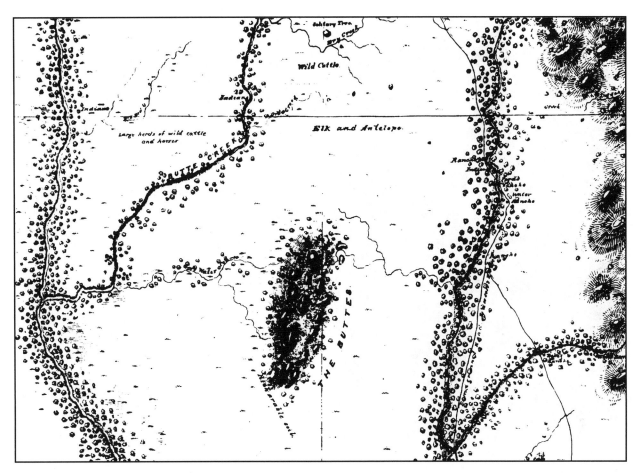

Indian camps and herds of wild cattle, horses, elk and antelope are shown on this map of 1849. Captain Riley, U.S. Expedition.

exchanging tools, guns, fabrics and beads for pelts.[11] Tasu'mili told of the tall white men in strange, bright-colored clothing who came to Pakan'yani when she was a small child. They spoke a language that the villagers could not understand, but the men brought out their bobcat, cougar and beaver furs and traded them for strands of beads, tools and blankets. Tasu'mili treasured a small string of brilliant blue and white trade beads given to her by an aunt, an elder in the tribe.[12]

A hidden enemy stalked the Indians, however, as the malaria spread; they had no immunity to this disease. Adding to the calamity, the floods produced an explosion of the population of *anopheles* mosquitoes that spread malaria to every tribe. The diaries of the American explorer J. J. Warner describe the tragic results.

The banks of the Sacramento River, in its whole course through its valley, were studded with Indian villages. On no part of the continent over which I traveled was so numerous an Indian population. [1832]

On our return, late in the summer of 1833, we found the valleys depopulated. From the head of the Sacramento to the San Joaquin, we did not see more than six or eight live Indians, while the large numbers of their skulls and dead bodies were to be seen under almost every shade tree.

Though epidemics had occurred before, never had they been so severe. An estimated fifty thousand native Californians died, and by the late 1830s there may have been only fifteen hundred people in the Maidu nation. Seven of every ten had perished.[13]

Pioneers pulled, pushed and sometimes dismantled their wagons to get over the mountains.

Tasu'mili was only six years old at the time, and she and her father lived through the epidemic. There is no record of how many others were left alive in Pakan'yani, but survivors from other groups gathered there and continued their way of life as well as they could. The long distances between occupied villages made it even more difficult for them to maintain trade and social exchanges. Many of the elders had died; the songs and tales of thousands of years were lost and the lines of countless generations were broken. The survivors kept the traditions, songs and legends that they remembered and passed them on to their children.

Leaving California behind them, the brigade of John Work struggled toward the fort. Nearly three-quarters of the people were ill; "only 2 women in the camp clear of the fever," wrote Work on August 23.

Saturday, August 24. The greater number are very bad and 7 more are taken ill during last night and today, making in all 72 people ill. Our case is becoming more alarming every day. Our only chance of escape is to push on to the fort and a long road it is, at the rate we can possibly march, at least a month's march, but we must push on as it is our only means of safety.

It took two months before they reached Fort Vancouver, October 31, 1833. Five people had died of malaria and one of injuries. In his report to the company directors, John Work wrote,

Notwithstanding all our trouble and difficulties, I am sorry to inform you . . . our hunt only amounts to 1023 beaver and otter skins, indeed the country is now so exhausted that little can be done in it.[14]

The expeditions from America and Hudson's Bay Company continued, however, although the beaver became still more scarce and the pelts were losing value. The Mexican government increased its demands on the hunters and required that they become Catholics and citizens of Mexico to apply for passports and licenses. The men arranged for quick baptisms and married Mexican girls, or ignored the whole procedure. Some were arrested, their furs impounded, and they lost their entire year's wages.

The Mexican government was anxious to have the land settled by those who would swear loyalty to Mexico, and the governor was empowered to make grants of hundreds of thousands of acres of land, as the Spanish had before them. These grants covered vast areas of the valleys and foothills, reaching as far north as Redding near the Oregon Territory, and included the ranchos of Bidwell and Sutter.

The United States, meanwhile, had grown increasingly interested in California and its strategic harbors on the Pacific Ocean. President Polk launched a campaign encouraging people to go west and settle the land, convincing them that it was America's "Manifest Destiny" to occupy and own California. The pioneers were driven not only by loyalty to their country, however, but by a severe economic depression and a desire for land.

In 1841, the first group of immigrants from the United States crossed the continent and arrived at Sutter's Fort, where they were given shelter before heading out to begin their new life. More groups followed. The Grigsby-Ide wagon train started out in 1845, and Joseph Wood, his wife Polly and their children left their home in Ohio and joined the group. These pioneers planned to settle in California and Oregon and work the land. According to the Wood family, Polly and all their children were killed in an Indian attack on the Humboldt River, in Nevada Territory. The wagon train continued its journey to Sutter's Fort, where Joseph's arrival was noted in the records. In 1846, Joseph Wood did the unthinkable—he went back across the plains to Ohio. Only a few people are known to have made that dreaded trip a second time; others who returned traveled by sea, either around the Horn or crossing the Isthmus of Panama.

Still more pioneers came west. The horrifying experiences of the members of the Donner party, trapped by early snows in the high Sierra in 1846-47, were soon known in every country. But even as the chilling story of cannibalism was retold, families sold their farms and businesses and packed their wagons to begin the same journey.

The United States was gaining a stronger grip on California. By 1846, the government had pressured Britain to give up its territory south of the present Canadian border without a struggle. Not only was the game nearly depleted, but beaver hats were no longer popular. The fashion that had lasted nearly two hundred years changed, and beaver pelts that had sold for six dollars each in 1832 brought only a dollar in 1842. The Hudson's Bay Company abandoned the California expeditions. On the coast, Russian colonists and fur traders had hoped to lay claim to the land, but when the fur animals were gone, they, too, left California.[15]

The competition for the territory was now solely between Mexico and the United States, which were at war over the Texas-Mexico border. Neither paid heed to the plight of the native Californians, who were left with scattered people, desolate villages, and only remnants of the once great herds of wild animals.

Trapper on horseback; by Frederick Remington.

John Sharp, a miner armed with a pistol and a pickaxe. Courtesy Bancroft Library.

Chapter Three
MINERS AND MERCHANTS
1848-1849

Monday, January 21, 1848
Some kind of metal was found in the tail race that
looks like gold.
—HENRY BIGLER, SUTTER'S FORT

W HEN JAMES MARSHALL found a few
nuggets at Sutter's Mill on the Ameri-
can River, it seemed of little importance at first. The
discovery "did not impress me," wrote Theodor
Cordua, after seeing the tiny flakes of gold dust at
Sutter's Fort. Only nine days later, at the end of the
Mexican-American war, the Mexican government
relinquished its claim to the territory and ceded California to the United States as part of the Treaty of
Guadalupe Hidalgo. "All sham . . . got up to guzzle
the gullible," said the editor of the *California Star*,
refusing to believe the reports of the discovery of
gold.

Sam Brannan, the storekeeper at Sutter's Fort,
had seen the nuggets and recognized the implica-
tions. It was his chance to get rich, but not by
mining. He set up a store of his own in the hills on
the river near Sutter's Mill and bought up all the
picks and shovels and every iron or tin pan he could
find for twenty cents each. Then he rode to San
Francisco and went up and down the streets waving
a bottle of gold, shouting "Gold! Gold on the American River!" He did not have long to wait.

Soldiers abandoned their posts in San Francisco
and Monterey, and sailors jumped ship to rush to
the American River. Men poured out of Sutter's
Fort, leaving the tanneries, bakeries, blacksmith
shops, distillery and mills empty. They bought the
pans from Brannan for sixteen dollars each, and
helped themselves from Sutter's food storehouses.
On the ranchos, the men left the livestock to fend
for itself and dismantled the ranch homes and barns
for makeshift mining equipment. By the time Jonas
Spect found the first nuggets on the Yuba River a

few months later, Sam Brannan had made over
$36,000, and thousands more men were on their
way to the hills.

> *When I arrived at a point on the Yuba River a*
> *little above Timbuctoo Ravine, I washed some*
> *of the dirt and found three lumps of gold worth*
> *about seven dollars. I pitched my tent here on the*
> *night of June 2, 1848. In about a week I moved*
> *down the creek and remained there until*
> *November 20, when I left the mines forever.*
> —Jonas Spect

Jonas was one of very few men who did not catch
gold fever.[1]

Governor Mason, who was in charge of the
California Territory, bought about 230 ounces of
gold from the miners, packed it in a tea caddy, and
sent it to President Polk by ship, along with his
report on the situation. The gold got immediate
attention, and on December 5, 1848, President Polk
announced the discovery in his address to Congress,
while displaying the tea caddy full of nuggets.
"GOLD IN CALIFORNIA," trumpeted East Coast
newspapers, detonating a worldwide explosion.
There had been gold rushes before to other areas of
the world, but never had so many joined the race.

People rushed to California from every corner of
the world to seek their fortune. Men sold their possessions or borrowed money and left their families,
homes and jobs for the chance of becoming rich.
The United States was in a deep depression, and
for many without jobs this seemed a way to get out
of debt. It was the lottery of the age, fanned by

newspaper accounts of how easy it was to pick up nuggets and come back a wealthy hero. The majority did not plan to stay in that distant place, but intended to gather the gold and return home as soon as possible. Sailors, lawyers, farmers, ministers, outlaws and merchants speaking a dozen different languages headed for the California Territory. By the end of 1848, men had arrived from Mexico, Hawaii and Canada, and two-thirds of the adult males in Oregon had left for California. Next came the hordes from the East, traveling by cart, wagon and on foot across the wilderness. They came by ship from Australia, China, England and Europe—from almost every country in the world. Hundreds of ships lay rotting in San Francisco Bay as men abandoned them to dash to the gold country, and valuable cargoes of cowhides, tallow and pelts from California ranchos disintegrated in the holds.[2] More than forty-two thousand people came overland in 1849, counted by the incredulous military men at several forts along the way. If they were fortunate, two thousand miles and six months later they reached California, worn and exhausted, skin black from the sun, teeth loosened by scurvy and supplies spent. The overland trails, however, brought them into the heart of the gold country.

The thirty-nine thousand travelers who arrived by sea that year were pale and weak from weeks of crowded and filthy conditions, poor diet, cholera and scurvy. To their dismay, instead of stepping off the boat into the gold country, they found they still faced a journey of hundreds of rugged miles.

I have seen plenty of chaps that just came in, coming up into the hills with their dunnage on their backs, hanging down behind, but their faces was hanging down longer forward.
—J. A. Manter

FOR

CALIFORNIA!

Mutual Protection
Trading & Mining Co.

Having purchased the splendid, Coppered and very fast Sailing

Barque EMMA ISIDORA,

Will leave about the 15th of February. This vessel will be fitted in the very best manner and is one of the fastest sailing vessels that goes from this port.

Each member pays 300 dollars and is entitled to an equal proportion of all profits made by the company either at mining or trading, and holds an equal share of all the property belonging to the company. Experienced men well acquainted with the coast and climate are already engaged as officers of the Company. A rare chance is offered to any wishing a safe investment, good home and Large profits.

This Company is limited to 60 and any wishing to improve this opportunity must make immediate application.

An Experienced Physician will go with the company.

For Freight or Passage apply to 23 State Street, corner of Devonshire, where the list of Passengers may be seen.

JAMES H. PRINCE, Agent,
23 State Street, corner of Devonshire St., Boston.

For further Particulars, see the Constitution.

Propeller Power Presses, 142 Washington St., Boston.

Poster advertising passage by sea to California for $300, leaving around February 15, 1849.

From San Francisco, men jammed aboard whaleboats, scows and rowboats heading up the Sacramento to the Feather River, and then to Marysville, where they spilled onto the waterfront. They traded and hustled their way into the hills, on pack animals if they could afford them, but otherwise on foot with their possessions strapped on their backs.

There were fortunes to be made if the prospectors could recover from the overland or sea trip. In 1849, gold was so plentiful that fist-sized nuggets could be picked up from stream beds without turning a shovel, dug out in chunks with a spoon in some places, or pried from crevices with butcher knives in others.

A great many men were not content to work in one spot, but dashed from one dig to another at every rumor of a new strike, always hoping to stake a richer claim. Major Downie, who founded the town of Downieville, tells how he and his partner worked a claim on Poorman's Creek and were taking out $1,200 to $1,500 a day in "lumps weighing from a pound to twenty-five ounces each," but he left it when several men told him of a fabulous strike. It was only a rumor, and he returned to find that his partner had sold the claim for one ounce

*Miner on the trail;
by J. Ross Browne.*

($12) and the new owner "had taken $80,000 out of it, and meanwhile, I had swum the cold rivers, slept in the snow, been within finger-touch of an enormous fortune, and missed it."

Goods were scarce and prices rose to outrageous heights. Merchants quickly followed the news of big strikes into the wilds, and sold some items for their weight in gold. An old hen and rooster brought across the plains were purchased by Thomas Mooney for $100. They were the only ones in the county for a time, and were known as the "pioneer chickens." In a few short years, they made a fortune for their owner. The roosters that hatched were bought by miners for their shooting contests for $25 each, no doubt ending up in a cooking pot after the competition. The hens' eggs sold for a dollar each.

Said Mooney,

> *Why, I could no more count up the money
> those chickens . . . made for me than I could fly.
> Taking what I received for the young chickens, the
> eggs and the other goods I sold to those who came
> to see the shooting matches, for instance, ...
> I made thousands of dollars.*

Gold was so plentiful that the price stayed around $12 an ounce; regardless how much a man found, most of it went to pay for food, equipment and clothing. As droves of prospectors came looking for "easy pickins," gold flowed out of their hands and into the merchants' pockets. It was a wild and unpredictable market. Picks and shovels might be

Miners work a claim, shoveling dirt into the long tom. Courtesy Chico State University Library.

selling for $20 each, blankets for $80, a can of peaches for $8, or a can of sardines for $16 when suddenly rumors of a rich strike would fly around the camp and two thousand men would be gone by morning, the camp empty. Another merchant arriving with loaded mules, would find that his goods were nearly worthless. Like anyone else, a merchant could be rich one moment, penniless the next.[3]

Like Sam Brannan, Isaac E. Brown was a successful merchant. He arrived in California from Maine in 1849, and opened a blacksmith shop in a tent in Marysville. There was a shortage of hay for stock, so he bought $75 worth of scythes in Sacramento, hired men to mow great quantities of wild hay from the riverbanks and sold it for a good price. Then he followed the miners to a rich strike in Long Bar, a bend in the Feather River, and opened a store there.

With his profits he bought and sold land, making even more money.[4]

Another merchant was Charles O. Barker, twenty-nine years old when he left Vermont and joined the rush of 1849. He made his way to Marysville and followed the ridge between the Feather and Yuba rivers up into the Sierras, looking for a place to settle.

It was inevitable that the beautiful places occupied by the Indian villages would be the very ones the newcomers desired. Each village was located on a southern slope with open meadows and abundant water. Maidu villages throughout the area were swallowed up in the great rush for gold.[5] Pakan'yani was no different—it lay directly in the path of the gold-seekers. Barker claimed 160 acres to one side of the village, and soon the freshly split posts of his corrals encircled the meadow.

Barker House appears on this map of the Feather and Yuba rivers, published in 1850. The Upper Sierra is shown as "unexplored regions" with "perpetual snow."

The Maidu living at Pakan'yani managed to co-exist with the prospectors in what seems to have been an uneasy peace. There were no gold deposits at the village site and this may have been a factor. The chiefs and Barker may have worked out an agreement, since the Maidu could furnish valuable labor. Tasu'mili was by now a young woman of twenty-three years and still lived in Pakan'yani.

Many of the Maidu villagers worked for the miners, who turned the two nearby creeks inside out in their search for gold. Barker named the creek that had its headwaters below the village "Indian Creek," because of the presence of the Maidu. The other stream was named "Slapjack Creek" after the pancakes the miners cooked in heavy skillets over their fires. Downie described the smell of slapjacks cooking while he was at Foster's Bar:

The perfumes of pork and slapjacks, arising from a hundred frying-pans, cause an odor, which could only be compared with all the soap

GOOD NEWS

FOR

MINERS.

NEW GOODS,

PROVISIONS, TOOLS,

CLOTHING, &c. &c.

GREAT BARGAINS!

JUST RECEIVED BY THE SUBSCRIBERS, AT THE LARGE TENT ON THE HILL,

A superior Lot of New, Valuable and most DESIRABLE GOODS for Miners and for residents also. Among them are the following :

STAPLE PROVISIONS AND STORES.

Pork, Flour, Bread, Beef, Hams, Mackerel, Sugar, Molasses, Coffee, Teas, Butter & Cheese, Pickles, Beans, Peas, Rice, Chocolate, Spices, Salt, Soap, Vinegar, &c.

EXTRA PROVISIONS AND STORES.

Every variety of Preserved Meats and Vegetables and Fruits, [more than every different kinds] Tongues and Sounds; Smoked Halibut; Dry Cod Fish; Eggs fresh and fine ; Figs, Raisins, Almonds and Nuts; China Preserves; China Bread and Cakes; Butter Crackers, Boston Crackers, and many other very desirable and choice bits.

DESIRABLE GOODS FOR COMFORT AND HEALTH.

Patent Cot Bedsteads, Mattresses and Pillows, Blankets and Comforters. Also, in Clothing—Overcoats, Jackets, Miner's heavy Velvet Coats and Pantaloons, Woolen Pants, Guernsey Frocks, Flannel Shirts and Drawers, Stockings and Socks, Boots, Shoes; Rubber Waders, Coats, Blankets, &c.

MINING TOOLS, &c.; BUILDING MATERIALS, &c.

Cradles, Shovels, Spades, Hoes, Picks, Axes, Hatchets, Hammers ; every variety of Workman's Tools, Nails, Screws, Brads, &c.

SUPERIOR GOLD SCALES.   MEDICINE CHESTS, &c.

Superior Medicine Chests, well assorted, together with the principal Important Medicines for Dysentary, Fever and Fever and Ague, Scurvy, &c.

N.B.—Important Express Arrangement for Miners.

The Subscribers will run an EXPRESS to and from every Steamer, carrying and returning Letters for the Post Office and Expresses to the States. Also, conveying "GOLD DUST" or Parcels, to and from the Mines to the Banking Houses, or the several Expresses for the States, insuring their safety.——The various NEWSPAPERS, from the Eastern, Western and Southern States, will also be found on sale at our stores, together with a large stock of BOOKS and PAMPHLETS constantly on hand.

Excelsior Tent, Mormon Island,   WARREN & CO.
January 1, 1850. | ALTA CALIFORNIA PRESS.

Advertisement promised great bargains at "the tent on the hill."

factories in Ohio, frying out at full blast. There was much sickness about this place at that time, and I do not wonder at it, for the smell of the place was enough to make anybody feel out of sorts.[6]

The new Californians represented a great many cultures and races suddenly thrown together, and the place names they chose reflect that diversity. They used the Spanish word for a parcel of property, calling it a "rancho" or ranch. They established general merchandise stores, rather than the trading posts common in southwest and northwest America. There were no outposts, the gold miners having beaten the military to the hills. Hotels were called "houses," e.g., Barker House, New York House, and Columbus House. Every settlement, no matter how many tents or buildings it comprised, was called a town, not a village. Only a few places in the area were given Indian names, such as Yuba, Concow and Honcut. Many were given vividly descriptive names: Poverty Hill, Sucker Run, Jackass Flat, Humbug and Slapjack. Cuteye Foster's Bar was not a saloon, but a bar of rich, gold-bearing gravel on the North Fork of the Yuba River, first occupied by Foster, a rough-looking character with a cut above his eye.[7]

Thousands of men traveled the pass between the Yuba and Feather rivers, many of them needing shelter and food. Barker erected a roadhouse, which was actually a large tent, and the place became known as Barker House.[8]

In his journal of 1849, William J. Organ recalls traveling four or five hours on horseback from Little Grass Valley toward Marysville:

We came to a place where preparations were in progress for a roadhouse, to accommodate the rapidly increasing travel. The bar was already doing business under some large pine trees.[9]

The original Barker House had a rough wood frame, probably made of logs, with canvas roof and sides. Merchants tried to save a good piece of wood for a sign, but if necessary they cut out a piece of canvas, painted it, and nailed it to a tree. There were

A night's lodging within the fence offered little except shelter from traffic on the trail; by J. Ross Browne.

few mills in the area, and those were abandoned as workers headed out to look for gold. The mills were then picked clean for any usable pieces of wood, iron and machinery. Lumber was so scarce that it sold for up to $650 per thousand board feet. Packing crates and old dry goods boxes sold for two or three dollars each, and were used to make floors in the tent houses; otherwise, the floors were hard-packed earth. Sacramento, San Francisco and hundreds of towns in the Sierra Nevada were tent cities; in April of 1850, Marysville was a city of three thousand tents, some of them two stories high.[10]

Back in the States, Congressmen argued heatedly about bringing California into the Union. It had been a United States territory for only a few weeks, and some felt that its vast riches were compelling reasons to move fast. But the balance of the Union

with respect to slavery was about to be upset. There were fifteen northern states voting for statehood, and fifteen southern states in bitter opposition, since California was anti-slavery for the most part. In the California territory, opinions varied, depending on the home state of the settlers. Twenty-five miles from Barker House, the small town of Rough and Ready aligned itself with the Confederacy, declared itself the "Republic of Rough and Ready," and seceded from the Union five months before California was even a state.[11] Gold from the area went to the Union anyway, although the town did not officially join the United States until 1948.

While the politicians fought, the Forty-Niners dug up every stream and river, turning over every rock. There was little or no government, so the miners made their own laws in the midst of the chaos.

A prospector washes out a panful, hoping for nuggets.

Groups of men formed companies, following business procedures. They adopted bylaws, voted on rules for staking mining claims and carefully registered them with the newly elected *alcalde* of the camp; sometimes claims were also registered with the *alcalde* in Marysville.[12] Punishment for theft varied from place to place. One group might hang a man for stealing tools, another brand a mark on his cheek. Lashings were a common punishment, and were often severe enough to cause death.

Perhaps because of the severity of the punishments, there was relatively little crime in the early days of the Gold Rush. Many diarists note that during the summer of 1849 there was no need to lock up their goods, which was fortunate since most of them camped out on the rocks, or lived in tents and brush huts. Very few took time to cut logs for a cabin. Throughout the Sierra, tools left lying on a stream bed were recognized as the mark of a claim on that spot.

As races and ethnic groups mingled, prejudice raged. Every group—Chinese, South and North Americans, Germans, Mexicans, Hawaiians, and Irish—had its own idea of who belonged in the territory and who was "foreign." Major Downie, who was himself Scottish, described seeing such a group on the march near Bullard's Bar:

> *The company consisted of from twenty to thirty men armed with pistols, knives, rifles and old shotguns. I was told in tip-top Tipperary brogue, that the expedition had set out with a view to driving away all "foreigners." The crowd was a motley one—the Irishmen were marching to*

drive off the Kanakas. They were joined by Dutchmen and Germans who could not speak a word of English. Then there were a few New Yorkers, all had joined in the alleged common interest of protecting the native soil . . . against the invasion of "foreigners."

Downie was unable to find out what the group accomplished, or how they determined who was a "foreigner."

On September 9, 1849, after only seven months as U.S. possession, California was admitted to the Union as the thirty-first state. The United States assumed ownership of all lands. Each land grant given during Spanish and Mexican rule was examined; almost all were affirmed.[13] But those ranchos in the path of the gold-seekers were in turmoil, as miners overran the land, stripped the mills and buildings, and shot the cattle. Where a year before only two thousand had been working the rivers along a two-hundred-mile stretch of the Sierras, now hordes of men—between 81,000 and 89,000—scoured for gold. In the Barker House area, miners were so numerous that each claim was limited to a ten-by-ten-foot square.

The Indians' rights and interests in the land were ignored. Not only were they vastly outnumbered by the newcomers, but, typical of every conquest in history that either annihilated or enslaved the native people, they were also considered a menace to be eliminated.[14] Some tribes fought when pushed aside, but the Maidu gave little resistance. Moreover, since they believed that man does not own land, but is given only temporary use of it, they believed that they were lending the land to the white men.

Those who had survived the great epidemic of 1833 now faced even greater horrors. They were hunted, assaulted and killed. Their children were taken alive and sold as slaves. Their food sources were ruined. Streams were muddied and fouled, and every inch of every streambed was occupied by a miner ready to fight to the death anyone who came near his claim. The Maidu could not fish for trout and salmon, nor gather mussels. Summer was a crucial time for hunting game and gathering acorns to dry and store for the winter, but now it was difficult just to find food each day. The circle of creation was broken. Many who had resisted contact with the newcomers now had to work for the miners or merchants in order to escape starvation.

When a tax of $20 per month was levied on "foreign miners," the Indians were sometimes hired to collect it from the Chinese; by J. Ross Browne.

The miners had hoped to work at least into October, but the weather changed early in 1849. On September 9 the rains began, pouring down and gathering in the streams and rivers. The miners watched helplessly as flumes and races were ripped away. They heard the incredible sound of boulders the size of houses churning down the canyons, grinding everything to pieces. Men who wanted to save every speck of their gold for their return home chose to spend that winter in the canyons just above the high water. It was miserably cold, wet and lonely, but far cheaper than living in the valley towns.

Some stayed along the ridges, and that year Barker House and all the surrounding tents and sheds were filled with miners who had only their bedrolls, cooking gear and a shrinking bag of gold to see them through the winter.

Those who fled from the hills counted themselves fortunate to have escaped the snows, which were recorded at depths of twenty-five to thirty feet. In the high country, many miners starved to death because pack trains could not get through with supplies. One group attempting the trip just before Christmas was trapped in a pass high above Barker

The "Miners Coat of Arms" included tools, a battered hat, worn—out boots and fleas; by Britton and Rey.

Pack train in a snow storm, by Charles C. Nahl.

House, and sixteen men froze to death along with their sixty mules. Those in the valley lived through one of the worst floods of the times. In the winter of 1849–50, Marysville and Sacramento, which are built on natural floodplains, were deep under water. Nevertheless, the enthusiasm of some was almost beyond belief. People paddled around in boats, buying and selling land that lay under ten to twenty feet of water.

All sorts of means are in use to get about —bakers' troughs, rafts and India-rubber beds. There is no sound of gongs or dinner bells in the city. The yelling for help by some men on a roof or clinging to some wreck, the howling of a dog abandoned by his master, the boisterous revelry of men in boats who find all they want to drink floating free about them, make the scene one never to be forgotten. After dark we see only one or two lights in the city.
—Jacob Stillman

Anything that floated brought a good price; a whaleboat rented for $30 per hour and sold easily for $1,000.

When the water subsided, food was scarcer and prices higher than ever. The miners spent much of their precious hoard of gold on living expenses, and many died of cholera, which swept through the towns as the floodwaters receded, exposing heaps of rotting goods and animal carcasses. Scurvy was a dreaded and common disease throughout the mountain regions because fruit and vegetables were not available. Edward Gould Buffum described his symptoms:

> *Swelling and bleeding of the gums, followed by a swelling of both legs below the knee, which rendered me unable to walk. For three weeks I was obliged to feed upon the very articles that had caused the disease, and growing daily weaker, enduring the most intense suffering from pain in my limbs which were now becoming more swollen and turning black.*

His friends found a place along the trail where a sack of beans had spilled and sprouted during the winter. Along with the greens, they gave him tea made from the bark of fir trees, and Buffum slowly recovered.[15] Some of the miners stripped leaves from shrubs and cooked them into stews to survive the winter.

It was summer before the miners could return to the canyons in 1850. The water levels were high from the melting snow pack, and camps, equipment and rough cabins had vanished. Diversion dams had been torn away from the river beds, and the elaborate systems of flumes and ditches had to be built again. The old miner's ditch that still winds around the edge of the Woodleaf meadow is only a small part of a huge, ninety-mile waterway. That project was the work of Jacob Bartholomew and De Witt Clinton Gaskill of Forbestown, who formed the South Feather Water Company and hired Chinese laborers to dig the channels.[16] The campsites, cooking utensils, broken tools and pottery of the Chinese can still be found along the route, which ran from

Log dam built on Lost Creek by the South Feather Water Company. Photograph by Peterson-Bean.

the log dam on Lost Creek to Forbestown, and later, nearly to Oroville. The company sold water to mining companies. By 1857, nearly twelve million dollars had been spent in the construction of 4,405 miles of such systems in the Sierras.

Gold fever did not subside in 1850—36,000 more men came by sea while another 55,000 traveled overland.[17] The letters that had trickled back from the miners had not discouraged them. In fact, some thought that the descriptions of horrible conditions and back-breaking work were only ruses meant to keep others from enjoying the bonanza.

On their trip to California, the new gold-seekers passed more than 30,000 miners heading back home, some rich, but most of them entirely disgusted, with nothing but memories to show for their efforts.

Top: *Drawing of a miner, by John J. Audubon.*
Bottom: *"I am glad to hear that Mr. Emory has concluded to come to California, but I fear he will wish himself back in Michigan before he has traveled many days on the plains," wrote G. S. W. Twogood after his arrival in California.*

Detail of the painting, Sunday in the Mines, *by Charles C. Nahl.*
Courtesy Crocker Art Museum.

Chapter Four
FOOL'S GOLD
1850

Men are flocking like sheep from here, leaving good claims in anticipation of the rewards at the lake.
—PLACER TIMES, JUNE 17, 1850

IN 1850, strange stories spread about Captain Thomas R. Stoddard, who stumbled out of the hills in January, nearly dead, carrying a large number of huge nuggets. He told of becoming lost along with his companions in the high Sierra during the fall, and finding a lake when they were desperate for water. When they fell down to drink, they were astonished to see large lumps of pure gold lying in the moss. He claimed that they were attacked by Indians, and showed a wound on his leg to prove it.

Stoddard had been roaming the area for some time trying to find the lake when he asked for shelter overnight at Organ's mining cabin in Union Bar. Stoddard complained to Organ he had been shorted about $400 when he and his companions divided the gold. "The pieces were so large that it was impossible to make an equal division, and I got the small pile." When asked where his companions were now, he explained, "They went to San Francisco and took passage on the first vessel that sailed for Australia." Organ wrote in his journal, "After breakfast the next morning our guest left, strong in the faith that he would yet find Gold Lake."

The story was not unusual in those days of rampant gold fever, but the huge gold nuggets in Stoddard's hands made his story different—here was tantalizing evidence of a truly great discovery. The tale of Gold Lake is recorded in many diaries kept by miners and merchants.[1] There are numerous variations, but most writers agree on the basic story.

In Marysville, crowds began to follow Stoddard day and night, begging him to lead them to the place. He finally formed a party of fifty men, charging them $200 per day each. Hundreds more clamored to join, offering large sums of money, and of course, there was no way to stop them from following, even if they did not pay him.

Isaac E. Brown had just sold his store in Long Bar on the Yuba River and was in Marysville in June of 1850 when he heard the story of the fabulous Gold Lake. He explained in an interview in 1879 that he didn't believe the tale but "saw an opportunity for trade and speculation." He loaded his wagons with provisions to sell and joined the group of between five hundred and a thousand men following Stoddard.

The editor of the *Placer Times* wrote on June 17, 1850:

> *Specimens brought to Marysville weigh from $1,500 down. Ten ounces is no unusual panful. The first party that left were assured of $500 average daily. In the second party were 200 men with 400 mules and provisions . . . . Men are flocking like sheep from here, leaving good claims in anticipation of the rewards at the lake.*

Stoddard started from Marysville with his party, followed by a rapidly growing, boisterous crowd. Several thousand half-crazed men surged around Stoddard, traveling up the ridge between the Yuba and Feather rivers, each trying to be the first to see the lake. Many started out with wagons, but once into the hills, there was only a rough trail and wagons soon broke down and were abandoned. Prices of mules and oxen soared as men tried to buy more pack animals from each other and from ranchos along the way. Some oxen were butchered on the

Packing into the mountains; by Charles C. Nahl.

spot, and the beefsteaks and ribs fetched high prices.

Brown's wagons must have been in good shape, because he made it as far as Barker House before they broke down. Since the place was ideally located for trade, he bought the property. He built a store and hotel and, contrary to the custom, he continued to call it Barker House instead of naming the place after himself. To further encourage travel, Brown organized a company, and within a few months his crews had chopped a thirty-mile road out of the rocky hills with picks and shovels, aching backs and blistered hands. It was the first road into the area, and it led straight to his public house.

The group following Stoddard continued up the pass, and Mr. Haven, an eye-witness, told of meeting this crowd.

I was traveling over the mountains with a companion on a prospecting tour, when one evening we made our camp at the base of a high hill. I ascended the hill to take a look over the country, and to my utmost surprise, found the valley alive with at least three thousand people. Calling my partner, we descended, and joined the throng. I found there a man with whom I had crossed the plains, and he pointed out to me Captain Stoddard, a Philadelphia gentleman, who had offered to conduct this crowd to new diggings at "Gold Lake," where, he had assured them, wealth untold could be found. For several days we traveled along and at last we came upon a lake nestled among lofty mountains.

"That is it!" said Stoddard. "There are tons of gold there!"

About four hundred men at once

Freight wagons and miners navigate a rough mountain trail.

started on a run. Within an hour it had became evident to several thousand men that they represented as many fools. There was not a sign of gold and expectations, hopes, anticipations suddenly turned to anger and a thirst for revenge of the most intense nature. "Hang him!" "I have a rope that will hold him!" "String him up!" Such were the exclamations mingled with imprecations that filled the air as hundreds of men made a rush for the Captain. We were persuaded that the man was crazy. So when the mob approached to seek vengeance on the unfortunate man, we drew our revolvers and told them that so long as we were able to defend him, no one in that crowd would be allowed to hurt a crazy man. That settled it, and although the poor fellow was made the target for a good deal of abuse, after this no further attempt was made to kill him.

The newspapers had been silent about the debacle, but on July 1, the *Placer Times* explained, "The entire matter was evidently stewed in the brain of a lunatic, and all Marysville was eager to hunt him, and elevate him socially, on the end of a rope."

The mob continued to explore the mountains around Onion Valley, and with a bit of wry humor, named one of the lakes in the area, "Gold Lake." Though they never found the lake of nuggets, they discovered other rich, gold-bearing areas. La Porte, Onion Valley, Whiskey Diggings, Poker Flat and the surrounding area eventually yielded more than one billion dollars in gold. Some believe that Gold Lake was all a hoax. But others believe that the fabulously rich Nelson Creek area may have been Stoddard's lost "gold lake." At Nelson Ledge the river cut through the quartz, exposing a gold vein five feet wide.

Settling a dispute in a mining camp of the 1850s; by J. Ross Browne.

The towns that had suddenly burst into life continued to thrive, many reaching populations of five to six thousand people, with banks, hotels, newspapers, libraries, breweries, bowling alleys, brass bands and merchants of every kind. Hat and boot makers, ministers, doctors, sign painters, barbers and lawyers are listed in the early census records.

Onion Valley became such an important freight station for all the high mines that for the next ten years Barker House and other property in the area was described in documents as being "on the trail (or road) from Marysville to Onion Valley."[2]

Stoddard never lost his belief in Gold Lake, and wandered from place to place telling the story. Major Downie said that Stoddard later joined his camp, where "he found protection against any attempts to annoy or hang him."

"Jan. 26, 1850, Men returned from their search after 'Gold Lake'—The lake could not be found but Nelson Creek was found, and three claims made. On the bank opposite upper claims took out in an hour or two over one hundred dollars in very coarse gold nuggets." From the journal of Charles Parke, courtesy The Huntington Library.

Protecting the Settlers, *by J. Ross Browne, 1864.*

Chapter Five
TURMOIL
1850-1853

*The Indians threatened to burn the Barker House . . .
and the whites built a fort at Oro Lewa for protection.*
—J. W. PRATT LETTER

IN OCTOBER or November of 1850, Brown sold Barker House to a couple of miners who had found gold on the river, Amos Hill and Cyrus Jumper, and sailed for Maine from San Francisco. He was one of those who managed to go back east a wealthy man.

On January 13, 1851, Cyrus Jumper took the opportunity to record his claim for land in Yuba County. The property was still called "Barker House" or "Barker Rancho."

Brown stayed in the East only a short time before he was drawn back to the wild adventures of California. When he returned in August of 1851, he built a hotel and store eight miles down the road from Barker House, along with a sawmill, at a cost of $8,000. He was still reluctant to name a place after himself, but when he sold the mill to Martin Knox and P. E. Weeks in November of 1852, they named the town in his honor, thus founding Brownsville.

By late 1851, it was harder to make a fortune quickly, and people were already talking about "the good old days" of 1849. California still held its allure, however, for the thousands more that came overland and by sea that year.

In the fall of 1851, twenty men met at Barker House to form a joint stock company, the Hampshire Company, "to engage in mining, merchandising, and lumbering." Their mill was finished in the spring of 1852, but by then the price of lumber had fallen to $100 per thousand board feet. Too many men had tossed aside their gold pans and shovels and gone into lumbering.

Cyrus Jumper was one of them. He sold his interest in Barker House to Amos and George Hill, and left to try his luck operating a lumber mill a few hundred yards down the road.[1]

Hotel management must have seemed a slow way to riches for the Hill brothers, too, compared to their adventures as gold miners, for on December 13, 1851, they borrowed $1,228.25 and invested the money in the Sutter Quartz Company mine. This sixteen-stamp mill in Forbestown was the newest method of processing gold-bearing quartz ore, and investors eventually poured $200,000 into it. By spring of 1852 the mine still had not paid off, but it seemed like such a sure thing that George and Amos mortgaged the "Barker House and fixtures situated on the Onion Valley Road leading from Marysville to Onion Valley" to Joseph T. Bickford, holding off creditors for a little longer.

By August, Bickford would wait no longer for his money, and sold the mortgage to Calvin Farr. Late in the year, the mine at last paid off for Amos Hill and made him a rich man. On November 22, he sold his forty-five percent interest, including "teams and wagons," for $8,000 cash to David Paige, fresh from San Francisco. With this fortune in hand, he left the area without paying Mr. Farr, leaving brother George to face the consequences.

Farr foreclosed on the Barker House mortgage on December 13, 1852. At the public auction the next spring, John S. Capron of Marysville successfully bid $1,200 for the property, and Sheriff Gray signed over the deed to Barker House and 160 acres. George Hill headed back into the canyons to look for more gold.[2]

With the constant change of owners, it was not

Sale of Certain Premises To Wit
"The Barker House and fixtures Situate on the
Onion Valley Road leading from Marysville

easy to keep peace between the people of Pakan'yani and Barker House. For the Maidu it was particularly difficult to see oxen and mules grazing in meadows that had been theirs for thousands of years, and to watch drunken men brawling where their house of worship once stood. Up to this time there had not been a major clash between the newcomers at Barker House and the Maidu, but when it came the results were tragic.

Thomas Kerns was killed by Indians only 400 yards from a ranch. A party of whites went out the next day to the Indian village and killed six or eight of the tribe. On Monday, G. B. Day, a minister of Mt. Hope, was found dead, with 17 arrows sticking into him. He had been thrown into the mining hole he was working. Citizens assembled in considerable number and went out to have revenge. They made a demonstration at the Indian village nearby, and were assured by the chiefs that the murderers would be given up.

Gravestone of Thomas Kerns.

The Americans returned with several prisoners, but whether they have the guilty parties or not is a question still to be determined.[3]
—Sacramento Union, February 2, 1852.

What brought on the first killing is not known. J. W. Pratt who was living nearby, described the events in a letter:

William Sherman, a native of Maine, started for the Barker House for provisions when he was murdered by Indians. Mr. Day of Mount Hope preached his funeral, the Indians believing him to be a big medicine man among the whites shot him full of arrows while he was working. Kerns was felled near Strawberry Valley and his partner escaped and gave the alarm. The Indians threatened to burn the Barker House and Oro Lewa and the whites built a fort at Oro Lewa for protection. They killed a number that were found in the woods but their names we never knew.

Kerns' grave is marked with a square-cut rock, his name hand-carved into the stone. It reads, "In Memory of T. Kern from Mo. Shot by Indians 1852 aged 24." Sherman and Day were buried at the southwest edge of the meadow of Barker House, and their graves were still marked in the early 1940s.[4]

When the Maidu killed Day by shooting him full of arrows, it may have been their repayment for the six or eight villagers killed by the whites, since a medicine man was considered worth more. Day was also well liked within the community of settlers, and for the Maidu the "most bitter revenge is . . . not to slay the murderer himself, but his dearest friend."[5] Pratt goes on to say: "Three Indians were hanged on a tree below Barker House. One boasted of help-

Justice was swift, sometimes final, during the 1850s.

ing kill twenty-two white men." A final note was written at the end of the letter by Albert August West in 1879: "The Indians were hung while others of their tribe watched from a distance. Two were taken down by the other Indians and burned in their burial manner."[6]

The peace had been fragile, at best, but now was shattered. Groups of armed men, rowdy and ruthless, roamed the hills, and the settlers feared them more than they did the Indians.

Though violence between the people of different races was rampant, not everyone was bent on destruction of the natives. Some miners and mer-

chants wrote of their horror at the actions of their comrades. William Swain wrote in his diary: "The miners . . . are sometimes guilty of the most brutal acts with the Indians . . . . Such incidents have fallen under my notice that would make humanity weep and men disown their race."

Newspapers articles pleaded for an end to the killings. United States agents wrote letters to their officers outlining plans for aid and petitioning the government to protect the native people. Eighteen treaties were drawn up in 1851 and 1852, which would have established Indian ownership of tracts of good land in return for their agreeing to cede the remaining ninety-three percent of California to the United States. The Maidu were to receive 277 acres along the Feather River around the Oroville area. The chiefs of most of the tribes signed them, but other Californians were outraged at the thought of returning even a small portion of the rich land to the native people. The furor reached the ears of the Senate, which refused to ratify even one of the treaties. The documents were hidden away in secret files and forgotten, and the Indians became refugees in their own homeland. They were not recognized as citizens of the United States, but neither were they aliens; thus, unlike the other ethnic groups and nationalities that overran the state, they could not become naturalized citizens. They could not own property and had no legal recourse, but became homeless wanderers dependent on any settler who would allow them to camp on his land.

A great many Maidu died in 1852 of disease, starvation and murder, and the village of Pakan'yani became still smaller. Tasu'mili, the young woman who had survived so many sorrows, was twenty-five years old. She took the American name of Nellie, and her father, Ya'lo, became known as Tom.

As the Maidu diminished, the settlers began to establish themselves in the new land. In 1852, a small family left the fort at Oro Lewa and moved back into their cabin at Barker House. Not many women came to California in 1849—less than eight percent of the population were women, even in 1850. Sarah Parlin, though, had sailed around the Horn in a windjammer with her husband in 1849. She and L. T. Parlin were merchants, and Amos and George Hill hired them to keep the store at Barker House. Sarah had another reason for wanting to get back to their cabin, aside from minding the store. She soon gave birth to a baby daughter, Clara, who is believed to be the first white child born in the mountain region of Yuba County. Later the Parlins moved to Strawberry Valley and kept a store. Sarah died when her little girl was only five years old, and is buried in the Strawberry Valley cemetery. Clara's father worked in stores throughout the mining region, and Clara herself lived until 1931.[7]

A Maidu woman, more than one hundred years old at the time this photograph was taken.

The arrival of a woman at a mining town and competition for her attention could strain the best of friendships.

In 1852, around fifty thousand more people came overland to California, including many wives and children. With them came the hope that their presence would have a civilizing effect upon the wild behavior in the mining country.

Despite a predilection for drinking and fighting, the miners had to put most of their energy and ingenuity into their work. While moving more and more earth to get to the deep deposits of gold, they developed a new strategy. Instead of shoveling the dirt into long toms, rockers, cradles or sluices and washing it, they forced the water through a nozzle and shot it against the hills, washing the dirt into the sluices and processing tons of earth in a fraction of the time. Hydraulic mining revolutionized the industry. It also mowed down entire mountains, sometimes coming within yards of towns and leaving them high on plateaus. Many people fled their towns as the miners approached, knowing that gold was worth more than their homes. The buildings

Hydraulic mining in upper Yuba County. Photograph by Peterson-Bean.

collapsed block by block, falling down the freshly made cliffs. The gold business boomed as mud washed down the streams and rivers, then ran into the Yuba, Feather and Sacramento rivers, and deposited up to eighty feet of silt in the bottom of San Francisco Bay.[8]

The business of hauling freight to the rich mining towns of the high country was one of the main sources of income for Barker House. By 1853, more than four thousand mules and four hundred wagons were involved in freight distribution to the mining camps in Yuba County. Jesus Bustillos of La Porte owned a string of 125 mules and employed numerous drivers. His crews loaded freight off the steamboats at the waterfront in Marysville, usually four to eight tons of goods and teams of six to twelve mules for each wagon. The freight included a half ton of barley to feed the teams during the five-day

trip to La Porte. Teamsters had regular stops at the hotels along the route. Barker House was the overnight stop for many of them at the end of the fourth day out of Marysville.

Gold production in California reached a peak of about 4,062,500 ounces in 1853 for a total value of $65,000,000 for the year.[9] Despite the advances in mining techniques, the processing of gold-bearing quartz proved far too costly for the amount of gold recovered, unless the deposit was unusually rich. Early in 1853, the Sutter Quartz Company owners finally realized that the stamp mill would never make money, and, hoping to recover some of their investment, they converted it to a lumber mill. They ran it for two years and then abandoned the whole operation. Amos Hill was lucky to have made any money in hard-rock mining, as other quartz operations were closing down throughout California.

Many began to recognize that, with so many people in the state, there wasn't enough gold to make mining worth while, and as they recovered from "the fever," they turned to agriculture. This was true not only in the fertile valley, but also in the hill regions. Settlers cleared the timber, and vast areas were planted with grain, grape vines and fruit trees. Ranches flourished with great herds of cattle, oxen, mules and horses.

Some of the meadows around Barker House were planted with wheat, and because of the high water table it grew well without irrigation. Most of the hills around the town were cleared of timber and fenced for grazing livestock.

Gold in faraway places still held its appeal. Another gold rush began in 1853 in Nevada. Historians estimate that 20,000 left California. Barker House was tossed from one owner to another—six within eight months. The price of the property went up and down depending on the gold strikes nearby. One owner, Charles Van Houten, kept it only four days before selling a half interest at nearly triple the price he had paid for the entire property. Unfortunately, he then sold a whole interest as well, and a year would pass before he could resolve the dilemma of that extra one-half interest.

Barker House owners in 1853:
1. Amos and George Hill, purchase price unknown
2. John S. Capron, $1,200
3. Charles Van Houten, $450
4. John R. Butler, half interest, $1,100
5. J. M. Abbott, purchase price unknown
6. Joseph and Susan Wood, $3,500 (included Abbott House)[10]

Freight wagons and teams; by Charles C. Nahl.

The earliest known photograph of Woodville House.

Chapter Six
THE GRAND HOTEL
1853-1858

The brick building is two stories high, erected by Joseph Wood on the main road at Woodville, now kept as a hotel.
—NORTH CALIFORNIAN, DECEMBER 5, 1857

JOHN M. ABBOTT claimed the land to the northeast of Barker House where the two trails to the valley converged. The Maidu *kum* had not been used since the killings earlier that year, and late in 1852 he built a house and barns near the site and fenced in the remaining meadows for his livestock. In the fall of the following year, the land was surveyed and it was discovered that Barker House was actually within his boundaries. It became Abbott's property, and the whole place with its two public houses was named Abbott House. Only a month later, in November, 1853, Joseph Wood, who had returned to California, became the new owner; the price had soared to $3,500.

Joseph Wood's life had never been easy. As a child, he had lost the sight of one eye after he was poked with a stick. He was orphaned at fifteen. Then, in 1845, when he was thirty-six, he suffered the loss of his entire family on the overland journey, and made the remarkable trip back across the continent. He married again, and in 1853 he came back to California with his wife, Susan, and her daughter, Alice, crossing the plains a third time. He moved to Abbott House, and, on November 4, 1853, a deed was recorded in the Marysville courthouse granting "Abbott House, all out houses, stables, corrals, household and kitchen furnishings including bar fixtures, blankets and cots" to Joseph Wood for $3,500. The deed also describes an enormous woodshed, sixty by eighteen feet, which gives a graphic picture of a Sierra winter and of the work required to put up the wood supply.

John M. Abbott invested the money from the sale of the property in the Lafayette House in Forbestown, sometimes called the La Fayette Mountaineer Hotel. Forbestown was by now the largest town in the area, with hotels, saloons, a brass band, doctors, Justice of the Peace, a water company, shoe shops and general merchandise stores.

Brownsville, too, was growing, as Isaac E. Brown and others sold off parcels of land to various merchants and businesses, and a lumber mill, cemetery, hotel, and shops were established.

Further up the pass, Strawberry Valley was a sizable town. Some lots were only twenty feet wide, just big enough to build a small shop. There were stores and church groups, a temperance guild, a cemetery, and a hotel.

Abbott House had begun in the same way as the others, but so far had not been split into parcels. A number of families lived there, operating the public houses, blacksmith shop, saloon and store, and raising stock—but there was still only one owner. It had a new name, however—now it was Woodville.[1]

Joseph Wood had not come to California for gold—he was a builder and a rancher. As soon as he and Susan signed the deed, he began to construct a barn on the site of the ancient Maidu *kum*. The barn was made of hand-hewn beams sixteen to twenty inches thick and fitted with mortise and tenon joints fastened by hand-carved wooden pegs. It measured fifty by eighty feet. Records show it could stable from one hundred fifty to two hundred oxen, mules or horses at one time, and freight wagons could pass one another down the center aisle. It was not unusual for sixty thousand pounds of freight to arrive in a single day, destined for delivery to the higher towns and mines. The freight

Joseph Wood, photographed at the Stinson Gallery in Marysville.

might include such diverse goods as a grand piano, steam engines, bolts of canvas, barrels of salted herring, silk dresses, shovels and books. The doors at each end of the barn opened onto the main road, enabling the wagons to drive through to unload goods and then continue on.

Freight teams continuously pulled into Woodville. Some arrived early in the day to unload goods, change teams, and head up the hill to the next town; others arrived in the late afternoon, their drivers ready for a big meal and a bed for the night. They were up by 4 a.m. to have a quick breakfast and hitch up their teams of ten to twenty mules. By 5:30 they had paid their toll at the tollhouse, then clambered onto the wagons, taking up the reins with shouts and whistles to steer the teams onto the road again. At times there were scarcely fifteen minutes between teams. The sound of harness bells and teamsters' calls from a departing team had hardly faded before another could be heard coming up the road. They generally traveled a few hundred yards apart to allow the dust to settle. Around thirty thousand people were living in and around La Porte, and they depended on these teams for all their provisions.[2]

Stagecoaches arrived with mail and travelers, weary from the rugged journey and thankful to step out briefly and stretch while the teams were changed for the last pull up the three-thousand-foot grade through Strawberry Valley to La Porte. On the stage trip down, the local banks and express companies at Strawberry Valley, Brownsville and La Porte entrusted their shipments of gold, bank drafts, letters and packages to the stage drivers.[3]

During this period, rumors of a National Wagon Road stirred excitement in the towns of Quincy, Oroville and Marysville, and in Hangtown in the central Sierra. Legislators in Sacramento were convinced that such a road would hasten the building of the transcontinental railroad, which would connect California to the rest of the United States. In the meantime, it would direct the flow of wagons into the state in a more orderly fashion. As it was, wagon trains struggled across the plains to California by whatever trail they could find. Congress appropriated money for the road and invited the cities at the end of each proposed route to present the advantages of their route for consideration. One route ended at Hangtown (Placerville), and the Humbug route ended at Bidwell Bar, near Oroville. The third, called the Beckwourth Route, crossed the Sierras through the Beckwourth Pass, then ran southward through Gibsonville, La Porte, and into Marysville by way of the Knox Turnpike, directly past the front door of Woodville House.[4]

Marysville and Oroville had been rivals from the start, and now they fought a bitter battle of words in the newspapers. In mid-summer, each group hired stagecoaches to travel its route and its opponent's, loaded with the men who were leading the fight. They passed each other in the high country and paused long enough to shout insults at each other before speeding off in opposite directions. The

Oroville Butte Record recorded the conflict:

> *The Marysville papers should call home their Commissioners, permit them to blow off the gas they have accumulated in their travels in a series of articles, and then 'dry up' on the wagon road question. If they can do nothing in favor of bringing the natural advantages of the northern portion of the State properly before the public, . . . they should cease their humbugging tomfoolery!*

Land values along the three routes began to climb, and merchants planned bigger stores and more shops as the campaign intensified.

Amid the extremely heavy traffic and wagon road rumors of 1855, Wood drew up plans for a grand hotel to be built near the Abbott House. He had learned brickmaking, masonry and carpentry from his father, who had built a large mansion in Ohio that the family ran as a hotel, coach station and tavern before his parents' death.[5] Joseph Wood worked as a builder before he came to California, and in San Francisco early in 1853. Now forty-six years old, he hired laborers to excavate clay pits and build large kilns in the south meadow to burn the brick. These were still standing in the early 1940s, approximately where the boat dock is today at Woodleaf. The

Top right: *Check from the Bank of La Porte.*
Bottom: *The stagecoach carried the wagon road commissioners over the proposed routes of the National Wagon Road.*

WOODVILLE HOUSE
FIRST FLOOR

One water line went to the beer cooler, then the water flowed to the outdoor wash basins, and finally to the old Abbott House behind the hotel where it was used to wash the laundry.

The second line supplied running water to the kitchen and the milk cooler.

Sink

KITCHEN

Wash basins

ONE-STORY COVERED PORCH

to Basement

Swinging doors

Beer cooler

OFFICE

Fireplace

Fireplace

SALOON

PARLOR

DINING ROOM

VERANDA

End walls 16" thick
Side walls 12" thick

SECOND FLOOR

The finest rooms were those on each end of the hotel which had fireplaces; the others were unheated.

These rooms could be engaged singly, or in a two- or three-room suite, and included the only upstairs room with double french doors leading to the veranda.

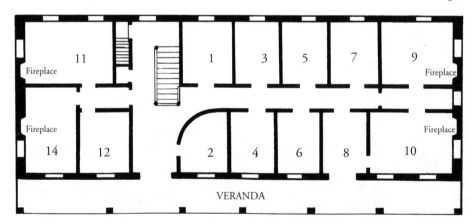

11   Fireplace   1   3   5   7   9   Fireplace

Fireplace   Fireplace

14   12   2   4   6   8   10

VERANDA

Room number was skipped. Many people refuse to stay in a room with the "unlucky" number.

Floor plan for Woodville House.

Drinks were bottled in crockery, and included ginger beer and mineral water, along with ale and beer. Imported from England in huge quantities, they provided ballast for ships.

brickmaking continued for months while the foundation was laid for a twenty-seven by eighty foot building. Freight wagons began arriving with lumber from the Hampshire Company, and windows, doors and fancy banisters from suppliers in Marysville. The main beams were cut and hand-dressed from Wood's timber forest. His descendants still own the elaborate set of planes used to fashion the moldings and trim.[6]

An ell was built at the back of the northeast end of the hotel to function as the kitchen, and contained a full basement. This wood frame structure adjoined the dining room, and was in use until 1943. The hotel is described in documents of the 1850s as a "brick house 80 x 27 feet on the ground, two stories high," with an "ell measuring 12 x 36 feet."

While building went on, the tangled property title continued to be unraveled. Former owner Van Houten discovered that the extra half interest in the property that he had sold to Butler was about to be auctioned at a public sale. Van Houten did not want that embarrassing surplus half interest to fall into anyone else's hands. He managed to buy it back, but at a reduced price—one-third of his selling price. One of the witnesses of the sale was his neighbor, Erastus Kellogg. Van Houten may have enjoyed needling Kellogg, for he then bought a long-overdue

note that a Mercantile Company held against Kellogg and promptly sued him. But Kellogg knew that Van Houten had sold Barker House and never paid off the mortgage, which was also long overdue. Kellogg bought the $450 mortgage and filed a suit to foreclose on Barker House, which by that time was called Woodville. Van Houten had met his match. He quickly settled with Kellogg, and when the details of his wheeling and dealing were finally completed, he seems to have left the area, for no more record of him is found.

Meanwhile, Joseph Wood kept building. On November 1, 1855, Isaac Pultz made the long trip to the Marysville courthouse to get the licenses to sell liquor and goods at Woodville House. The licenses were renewable in three months, and cost $15 for liquor sales and $7.50 for the sale of "goods."

In 1856, Wood petitioned the U.S. Post Office Department for a post office at Woodville, and in May it was granted, with Wood appointed the first postmaster. The U.S. mail service was still sporadic, and in some places mail was delivered only once a month. Most towns were also served by independent express companies that were much more efficient.[7]

By the fall of 1856, the brick construction of the hotel was complete and ready for interior finishing and plastering. Joseph and Susan Wood borrowed funds, then mortgaged the new structure and property in order to finish the hotel. Business was good, the prospects for future growth looked bright, and Wood had money coming in from reliable accounts.

On September 18, 1856, Wood hired David Doyle, a contractor and plasterer who lived at Oro Lewa, to plaster the interior of the hotel. He was promised $50 a month plus board and reimbursement for furnishing the lime and plaster. Samuel Jewett, Michael McGlennan, and A. C. Corbett were also hired that month to do finish work with molding trim, stairway balusters, doors and painting.

By the spring of 1857, the finish work was complete, and in April the freight wagons began arriving with loads of furniture and supplies from Scott, Vantine and Scott Company, a mercantile company in Marysville.

The hotel was truly grand—one of the largest brick buildings in the area. Inside the main double doors, the polished wood stairway led to the guest rooms. The windows were hung with velvet draperies and the rooms furnished with mahogany and ornate brass beds. In the evening the lamps were lit, and the guests gathered in the dining room and parlor on the first floor. The double doors at the southwest end opened into the bar, where a huge fireplace filled one wall. Comfortable chairs were drawn up around tables, each with a brass lamp in the center. At one end was an ornate bar with mirrors and a handsome clock; behind the counter, a deep sink with cold running water from the spring kept the beer chilled.

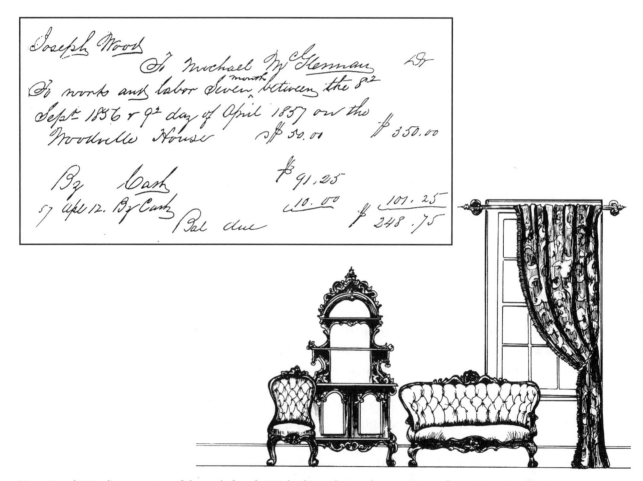

Top: *Joseph Wood's accounting of the work done by Michael McGlennan between September 1856 and April 1857.*
Bottom: *Furniture in the style of the 1850s included carved trim on sofa, chair and cabinet; heavy draperies were held back by a satin cord that was unhooked in the evening to cover the window.*

The main rooms were lighted with kerosene chandeliers; mirrors decorated the walls. On special occasions an orchestra was hired for dancing and entertainment; by J. Ross Browne.

The hotel's large third-floor room at the top of steep, narrow stairs was used as a ballroom on occasion, but was also the bunk room for miners and travelers unable to afford the fine rooms below. Here on a stormy night, as many as eighty men speaking a dozen different languages might try to find room to unroll their bedding on the floor. People of different colors, tongues and cultures crowded off the stages and wagons or came down from the upstairs rooms to the dining room and were seated around the tables. If it was cold, the choice places were those closest to the roaring fire in the large fireplace.

Through the swinging doors from the kitchen, waiters brought platters of beefsteak and fried chicken. Mashed potatoes were heaped high in bowls; green beans, gravy and trays of biscuits followed. Homemade preserves and fresh butter filled any empty places on the tables, and waiters cir-culated with pitchers of milk and pots of steaming coffee. The meal was usually completed with pie, pudding or cake, and cigars and brandy for the gentlemen. The cost was fifty cents.

Springs located high on a hill above Woodville were known from earliest times as an abundant supply of pure water. Isaac E. Brown had excavated a holding reservoir, still nearly intact below Woodleaf's present-day Town Hall, from which barrels of water were carried by wagon to the first public house.

Wood developed the system that provided running water inside the Woodville House. Logs were used to make pipes, and Charles Adams of Oro Lewa explained how it was done:

Logs ten feet long and one foot in diameter were cut from white fir or sugar pine. Through

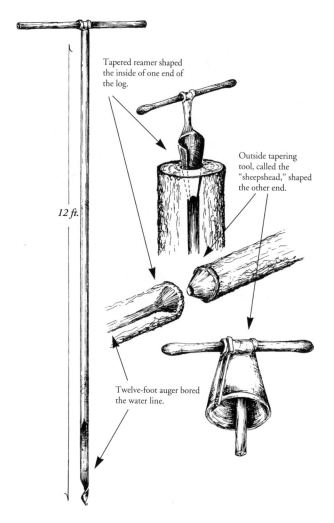

Tapered reamer shaped the inside of one end of the log.

Outside tapering tool, called the "sheepshead," shaped the other end.

12 ft.

Twelve-foot auger bored the water line.

these would be bored a three-inch hole by a twelve-foot auger. After eight turns, the bit had to be withdrawn and the shavings dumped . . . the logs were joined by caulking with oakum. After boring 900 feet of logs in the hot summer sun, I swore I would never do it again. But no water ever tasted sweeter than that which came from an ice cold spring through these moss-covered logs.

The log pipes ran southeast from the spring across the hill to a wooden water tank, then in a straight line down the hill to the hotel and fountain.

Piped-in water was a rare convenience in a hotel

in 1857, and because of the generous springs on the mountain, the Woods were able to add another touch. Using mining hoses with special fittings, they kept the road watered down. After hours, days or weeks on roads where dust as fine as flour lay six inches deep and nearby foliage was heavily covered, an arrival at Woodville was welcomed with cool, damp roads and a fountain spouting twenty feet into the air and splashing back into a pool.

The hotel's luxurious style, as well as its location midway between Marysville and the rich mines of the La Porte area, brought crowds of travelers from throughout the state. But 1857 also brought an economic depression to the area, despite the promise of the National Wagon Road. Many businesses failed, and when critical accounts owed to Joseph and Susan Wood were not paid, there were no funds to pay the final bills of the contractors nor the mortgages when they became due. By autumn, six lawsuits had been filed and three liens placed against the property.[8]

To complicate matters, the hotel was built astride the county line, and the suits were filed in both counties—two in Yuba County and four in Butte County. The sheriffs of both counties attached the same furniture and property.

Stories have circulated for 140 years about the hotel's placement across county lines. The bar was said to have been deliberately located in Yuba County where the sale of liquor was legal. The rumor is partly true—the bar *was* in Yuba County, but the sale of liquor was legal in both counties, and the hotel was built on that spot only because it was a good location.[9] Isaac Brown's road followed the ancient Maidu trail along the crest of the ridge, and marshy meadows dropped away on both sides. It was not only a convenient, but an unusually beautiful spot. Nevertheless, its location caused a nightmare for the litigators, who probably had no time to enjoy the view.

The battle between those who sought the property proceeded through the courts of Yuba County and Butte County. By late in the year, the Wood family could bear no more. Joseph Wood resigned his position as postmaster, loaded his family and belongings into his wagons, turned his teams onto

The National Wagon Road Guide, published in 1858, described traveling over the "living sea" of the prairie grassland, but did not mention that the route was well marked with cast-off goods, bones, broken wagons and graves, an average of seventeen per mile, and was little more than a trail for most of the way. It accomplished its purpose, however, of bringing more people to California.

the road, and left Woodville forever.[10]

Wood and his family sought peace in the beautiful rolling hills and rich meadowlands about twenty miles away, near his friend, John Abbott in Oregon House.[11] Joseph bought the 160-acre Bell Valley Ranch, which included a large house. He immediately began building another huge barn, remodeled the house into a hotel, and turned to raising livestock. He obviously had funds. Did the money arrive too late to satisfy the creditors, or did the

mortgage and lien holders refuse to settle? Had they only wanted to own the grand hotel themselves? We may never know, but back in Woodville, the battle continued.

Throughout the winter and spring a variety of people appointed by the sheriffs of Yuba and Butte counties came and went, trying to keep order. Most of the time they were able to keep the hotel, saloon, store, and post office running. They managed to tend the freight teams and livestock, and neighbors

1	Doz Bar Room Chairs
1	Bar Room Stove & Pipe
2	Tables
1	Iron Safe
1	Writing Desk
10	Tumblers
6	Decanters
1	Watering Pot
1	Water Tank Fancy
1	Clock in Bar Room
1	Looking Glass
1	Self Gold Scales
2	Flower Vases

Left: *Portion of Woodville House inventory, 1857.*

pitched in to help with the orchards and field crops.

Finally, on May 20, 1858, the District Court in Butte County declared that the "mortgaged premises or greater part thereof are situated in Butte County." The property would be auctioned in Butte County. Everyone expected the bidding to be fierce.

Meanwhile, the men in the state legislature finally made their decision on the route of the National Wagon Road. While Oroville and Marysville fought between themselves, Hangtown had found a more certain way to the politician's hearts. The merchants along that route raised the enormous sum of $50,000 to improve the road, and their route was chosen.[12]

The property values along the other two roads plummeted. A half-dozen men had been fighting to own Woodville in its choice location; now, no one wanted it. Even the U.S. Post Office Department withdrew its support, and the Woodville Post Office was closed.

When Sheriff Plum opened the bidding on July 12, 1858, the creditors had gathered, but there were no bidders. Finally the mercantile company, Scott, Vantine and Scott, made a bid and Woodville was theirs. The property, consisting of 160 acres, a fully furnished two-story brick hotel, saloon, store, bath houses and all fixtures, cottages, barns, stables, and corrals, valued at well over $20,000, sold for $1,600.

In those unstable times, the newspapers were full of stories of properties being sold to satisfy lenders—shops, ranches, hotels, toll bridges, homes. Court records tell similar stories, and the justice system did not always operate fairly. In 1850, the vast properties of John Rose, the pioneer for whom Rose

Bar is named, were sold to satisfy his creditors. His holdings included toll roads, ferries, toll bridges, ranches, hotels, stores, cattle and more than 4,500 acres. All was sold for only $410, the highest bid, to satisfy a debt of $4,122.35.[13]

Many lost homes and businesses because of economic changes and the development of new roads, but it was more common to lose property by fire. The entire town of Forbestown—hotels, offices, stores, restaurants and saloons—burned twice within eighteen months, and was rebuilt.[14] Woodville was one of very few towns that did not lose its main buildings through fire, but, because of the continuing change of ownership, it lost people with deep ties to the land, and the rarely attained stability that comes with long-term stewardship.

The hotel designed and built by Joseph Wood has a graceful style with an enduring appeal. Today the building's exterior design is recognized as unique in this region, and in 1975 it was accepted into the National Register of Historic Places. The architecture combines several styles, with the Georgian gabled parapets being the most unusual features.[15]

Although the dreams, labor, greed and sorrow of many people accompanied the hotel's inception, only the name of Joseph Wood has been recounted in prior histories. The town still bears his name— a tribute to a man of unusual vision and drive.

1855 advertisement for the wholesale suppliers to Woodville, now the new owners.

Lithograph by Aaron Stein, early 1870s.

Chapter Seven
THE TOLL ROADS
1860-1878

*The road . . . in a few days will be completed to the
Woodville House, where it will tap all the trade and
travel from the rich mining sections.*
—OROVILLE UNION RECORD, JUNE 3, 1865

WOODVILLE REMAINED in the hands of Scott, Vantine and Scott Company for two years. During that time the company may have recovered its losses. No doubt it was a burden, however, to continue to run a hotel so far from Marysville and the company's mercantile business. The company's banker, John Jewett, bought Woodville for $5,000 in June of 1860, but kept it only until October, and then sold out to brothers W. B. King and T. D. King for $4,000.

After the crushing loss of the National Wagon Road, Martin Knox of Brownsville formed a corporation to build a good road connecting Marysville and Woodville House. The Central Turnpike Company finished the thirty-seven-mile toll road in 1860, complete with gates and tollhouses at Challenge and Woodville.

The battle over the county lines still smoldered, and every year around tax time it intensified. The assessors from each county determined which items in the rooms of the Woodville House were on their side of the line, then tried to collect the taxes. Pity the person who shuffled the furniture into the county whose tax rate was lower.

It took an act of the state legislature to solve the dilemma. On April 15, 1861, the California State Assembly and Senate in the twelfth session passed an act changing the boundaries of Yuba and Butte counties so that the line "passing about three chains northerly of Woodville House, leave the same . . . in Yuba County."[1]

The supervisors in both counties immediately authorized new surveys and the publication of new maps. Yuba County surveyor Nelson Wescoatt got a first-hand look at the great brick hotel that had caused so much furor, and promptly bought a half interest in the property from the King brothers for $2,000.

By the spring of 1862, however, Wescoatt could no longer keep up with the demands of the hotel and of his county job, so he and the King brothers sold Woodville to his brother, Jonas Wescoatt and his wife, Amy. Jonas had been a California senator for two years, and Woodville may have seemed an ideal place to retire to the country life. Because of Woodville's stormy past, Jonas and Amy were quick to record the property under the protection of the Homestead Act.

Unfortunately for them, this maneuver was not enough. One of Jonas' friends who worked for the county had been indicted for secreting public funds, and Jonas helped post the $6,000 bond. When the man did not appear for trial, Jonas forfeited the $6,000, and Woodville was sold again.

The new owner was a young man from Ireland, James B. Kelly, with a love for whiskey and a hot temper. He arrived in California in 1851 and worked in many areas mining gold, getting into brawls now and then, but making a fortune in Sierra and Yuba counties. On August 18, 1863, Kelly paid $4,000 to the Wescoatts, and the deed was granted giving him "all claims to the homestead at Woodville." He kept his interest in the Blue Point Mine in Yuba County, however, as a hedge against hard times. Hotel-keeping and running the town of Woodville were just as risky as gold mining.

Over a period of thirteen years, Woodville had passed through the hands of thirteen owners

Kelly's bill from the Strawberry Valley store, 1860.

1 Gal. Whiskey
1 Pair Gum Boots
Files
1 Sack Spuds
20 lb. Cabbage
32 lb. Bacon
55 lb. Butter
100 lb. Flour
1 Nerve & Bone Liniment
1 lb. Black Tea
1 Sack Wheat
50 lb. Corn Meal
25 lb. Buckwheat
1 Sarsaparilla
1 Castile Soap
1 Gal. Whiskey

involving partnerships of twenty-two people. Strangely enough, Woodville remained one parcel. An increasing number of merchants and businessmen were active in freight, lumber and logging. The land was planted with fruit trees, wheat, corn, vineyards, berry patches and vegetable gardens, all of which were tended by field hands and gardeners. Beef and dairy cattle, horses, oxen and mules vital for transportation were pastured in large fields during the summer. The barns were filled with tons of hay for the livestock's winter feed, and stored many more tons of goods for people in the high country. All of this required stablehands, drovers and hostelers. A crew of woodcutters worked from early summer to fall, supplying wood for cooking, heating, washing, soap-making and iron forging, and filling the wood barn with firewood for the winter. The crowded hotel kept housekeepers, choreboys, cook and laundry workers busy. The owner of the town had a difficult job managing such a place

alone, but no parcels of land were split off and sold.

In 1863, the first settler on this property, Charles O. Barker, was assigned to serve on a commission with the Indian agent for the U.S. government to solve what the newspapers called the "Indian problem."[2] His task was to find all the Indians in an assigned area and take them to the reservations of Round Valley or Nome Lackee. The newspapers published tallies for each man, but Barker's name was not among them. He may have been one of those who refused to expel the Maidu from their land. Some federal agents, too, were appalled by the vicious acts of the citizens. Their letters to federal authorities pleaded for the government to protect Native Americans from murder and child slavery, but no help was forthcoming. The attention of the country was captured by the Civil War, and the problems of native people and the new Californians were again pushed aside.

A few miles away from Pakan'yani, the Maidu

families saw the agents coming.

My grandfather, . . . Alex Picayune's father and others ran up over the hill and crawled under a rock and hid. Soldiers came in with horses . . . burned all the bark houses down and . . . drove them out. They gathered all the Indians . . . herded them as they would sheep, over the summit and several old people died.
—Herbert Young[3]

Some of the Maidu retreated to remote areas for safety, and some were hidden by whites. Nellie married a gold miner from the East, Bob Kennedy, and they moved to Strawberry Valley where they were safe from the agents.[4] Many of the Maidu were taken to the reservations via a five-day forced march of suffering and death. While 461 Indians began the journey, only 277 reached Round Valley. In time, most of them fled the reservations and returned to their mountain homes.

By late 1864, Maidu families were back in their villages at Pakan'yani, Pomingo and Oro Lewa. Although they still could not own land, they rebuilt their homes and turned again to working with the ranchers and miners.

Yet another road was developed leading to Woodville that year: the Branch Turnpike or Rice's Road, which ran from Oregon House to Woodville. It was combined with the Central Turnpike and brought traffic from the Downieville, Camptonville and Grass Valley regions. Parts of that road are in use today as Oregon Hill Road and Indiana Ranch Road.

Competition between Oroville and Marysville was still fierce, and as the tremendously lucrative trade came down from the hills and went straight to Marysville, Oroville clamored for its own road. The Oroville-Woodville Pike was completed in 1865—the third main trade route connecting directly to Woodville. The men who ran the company could not work out an agreement with the Central Turnpike Company, however, and the two

Unloading freight at Woodville. Store at left; freight barn, center; hotel, right.

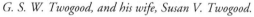

G. S. W. Twogood, and his wife, Susan V. Twogood.

roads ran parallel for several miles, in some places only six to eight feet apart, before finally coming together at Woodville.

OROVILLE-WOODVILLE PIKE NEARS COMPLETION

The hills, which have heretofore been the great "bugaboos" of teamsters, are no longer to be dreaded. Four, six, and eight-mule teams will have no more difficulty in passing over this road heavily laden, than they would on the best valley road in the state. Farmers in the Feather River valley will . . . [find] a ready, easy and profitable market for all their produce, and they can return with all the lumber, shakes or posts that their strongest wagon will bear up under. The road is completed to Forbestown and in a few days will be completed to the Woodville House, where it will tap all the trade and travel from the rich mining sections. We will soon be in direct stage, mail and express communication with this upper portion and can enjoy the benefits of these rich gold-bearing regions.

—Oroville-Union Record, June 3, 1865

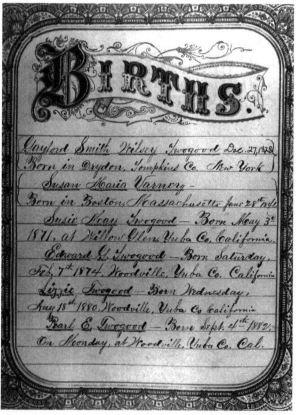

Page from the Twogood family bible, recording the births of Edward, Lizzie and Pearl Twogood, at Woodville.

The toll road between Woodville and Strawberry Valley was owned by James Birmingham, and in 1873, he hired a new man to take the job at the Woodville tollhouse. Gaylord Smith Wilsey Twogood and his wife, Susan, moved in on April 28, 1873. Twogood had come overland from Michigan in 1852 and eventually settled in this area after following the gold rush to the Fraser River in Canada in 1858, and the Salmon River in Idaho during 1862. He was a man of many talents. He had tried gold mining and photography, cooked in the camps on the rivers, hauled turpentine and rosin for the distilleries, tended store, delivered meat by wagon or sleigh, plowed fields for a large ranch, and made brake blocks for wagons. Beginning in 1856 and continuing for the rest of his life, he kept diaries in a small, neat script in leather-bound volumes. These journals form a remarkable record of his life, including his courtship of Susan Varney and the death of his friends. He described evenings with friends, helping neighbors round up lost cattle, a home burning down, his thoughts on the elections of presidents and congressmen, and traffic through town. After he and his wife moved into the tollhouse, he recorded the details of everyday living at Woodville for the next seventeen years.[5]

April 28, 1873. We trade some at Gaskill's store (Forbestown) then move to the Toll Gate House.

May 1. Commence taking toll, with business light. Quite windy.

May 4. Father Varney took dinner with us, first time in his life. Mr. Kingdon dines with us also.

May 21. We hear of the burning of Pine Grove House, kept by P. M. Cornell, Clipper Mills.

May 27. Is cold and windy. Mrs. Learmont died at 1 o'clock a.m.

June 5. We attend funeral of Eddie, infant son of Elmont and Jennie Brooks.

June 11. Pleasant. Father Varney gets turned out doors by his son's wife—comes down to stop with us.

July 4. This is the 97th anniversary of our nation's existence, which we celebrate this evening at a Grand Ball at Clipper Mills.

These were grand balls, indeed. Newspaper articles describe in detail the ladies' gowns, the long trains, lace and plume trimmings, long gloves, elegant hairdos and jewelry. Many of the men wore black ties, coats with tails and top hats.

The Twogood family on the porch of the Woodville tollhouse. Tollgate at left.

The stages that transported the celebrants carried gold as well, attracting thieves who lay in wait on remote stretches of the roads. There was Tom Bell, for whom Bell Valley in Oregon House was named, and Dutch Kate, a woman who terrorized the stages for a time before she was caught.

In August, 1875, the down stage from La Porte driven by Frank Morse was robbed near Forbestown by five men, who took the treasure box containing an estimated $1,800 in gold dust, $600 in coin.[6] Here are Gaylord Twogood's remarks about the robbery and other happenings at Woodville:

Woodville Toll House, August, 1875. We hear of the robbing of the stage below Robinson Mill (below Forbestown).

November 11. Mr. Kelly had a fight with a Chinaman, in which battle he came out second best.

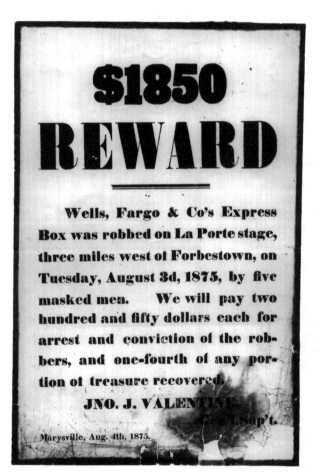

Reward poster describing the robbery of the La Porte stage.

January 20, 1876. Is cold and snow falls by fits and starts. I walked to the old barn, down to the old Barker place.

January 24, 1876. Josh Varney went to meet Morse (the stage). There is no road through the snow till Josh passed down on his way to Forbestown. Eve., the stage gets to Woodville about dark, and Morse stops here all night. The hog drovers stop here, Woodville, all night with 200 hogs.

January 29, 1876. The stage went up today, when it should have gone down. Mr. Butterfield and Miss Ida Pratt called on us. I read from the life of Christ, which I have been reading of late, during the storm.

February 19, 1876. Is pleasant—I go to Strawberry—took my first trip on snowshoes. Harvey Clark loaned me his. Eve., we meet in Lodge.

March 19, 1876. Sleigh got to Strawberry—could not get to La Porte, this trip. Snow has been 9-10 feet in Strawberry. Wife and boy and I dine at Emerson's.

March 27, 1877. About 1 o'clock we hear that old Dick, Richard Tennyson, Kelly's cook has killed himself by cutting his throat with a razor (in his room at the Woodville House). The following men were chosen as jury on the case—J. D. Worden, Edwin Adams, Samuel Thurston, Joseph Kirby, John Willey and G. S. W. Twogood. We all got through the night without sleep.

March 28. Is cooler. We put Tennyson in his coffin about 11 o'clock and the acting coroner takes charge for burial in Strawberry Valley. Eve., we retire early.

March 29. Is cloudy. Josh starts for Marysville. Wife washes. Mrs. Hall calls here. Rain falls quite fast for some time. Eve., snows some. I grind axe and a few other tools at Josh's.

August 10. Is warm. Our neighbor Kelly is very poorly—probably will not survive many months at the longest.

August 11. Kelly is no better, but gradually failing.

Monday, August 13. Wash Day. Mr. Kelly goes to Oroville and he probably will never see

Woodville again. He is very poorly.

August 15. Mr. Kelly's time on earth is likely very short.

August 18. Our boy has high fever.

August 20. Eddie is very feverish. I get uneasy and send for Dr. Mansfield.

August 25. Eddie is very sick—has a raging fever. We have to watch him night and day.

August 28. Eddie not well—thought he was going to die the latter part of the night, but he rallied again, and we hope again.

August 30. Eddie very weak but improving.

August 31. Mrs. Prindle goes home—has been here since Wednesday with us, and we are sorry to see her go.

September 2. Eddie rests very nicely. Wife is

Left: *Marysville-La Porte stage; the horses wear snowshoes.*
Above: *The mail was sometimes carried by dog team.*
Far right: *Skis (originally called snowshoes) were eight to fifteen feet long. Skiers sometimes nailed their boots to the skis to make sure they stayed on in downhill races, where they reached speeds of eighty miles per hour.*

The California Stage Company refused to list Woodville in its advertisements. Charles Barker had sued the company when a stagecoach carrying fourteen people on top turned over, crushing him. The company settled with Barker, but would not list Woodville, even though it was a regular stage stop, and was no longer owned by Barker.

worn out with anxiousness, and she has been sick one or two days since our boy was taken down.

September 7. Is warm again. We are nearly worn out, but it's all right if our boy only gets well.

September 10. Eddie is gaining slowly. Wife is very sick. I send for the Doctor. Mary comes down —is very kind indeed and does too much, in fact.

September 13. Is cool. Wife is some better after

a very restless night. Eddie gaining very slowly indeed. Glasner and Frank Parlin commence wood-chopping for Kelly.

September 14. Is rather warm. Eddie is dressed for the first time in about four weeks. Wife is more comfortable today. Mrs. Varney is here taking care of my folks—is very kind and attentive during our troublesome sickness. Mrs. Variel's baby is sick.

Typhoid, cholera, pneumonia, influenza and other illnesses took the lives of many people, but the Twogood family survived. Mr. Kelly made an unexpected recovery, and returned to his home at Woodville House, though he never completely regained his health. Neighbors and friends helped run the ranch and Woodville House, herding the cattle to pasture, rounding up the hogs, mending fences, and caring for his three children—Margaret (Maggie), Jeremiah and James.

By the late 1870s, a great deal of the land still in government hands was being used as summer range for cattle, hogs, turkeys and sheep. The stockmen, ranchers and their families joined the miners and lumbermen traveling up and down the pass, adding to the color and clamor at Woodville. The toll rates were:

Man on horseback	.25
Horse, buggy, and driver	.50
Two-horse buggy and driver	.75
Two-horse stagecoach	.75
Sheep per head	.03
Cattle per head	.02
Miner and pack animal	free

The stage running from Quincy to Oroville was robbed on July 25, 1878. Just five days later, the La Porte-to-Oroville stage was robbed by one man five miles below La Porte. Wells Fargo records show that gold specimens, a silver watch and the U.S. mail were taken. Twogood writes:

July 30, 1878. Stage was robbed near American House (below La Porte). Amount taken supposed to be $3,000.

August 11. Is very warm. I attend the funeral of an old and esteemed friend—father Albert of

Brownsville. He was in his 76th year.

September 6. Is warm during the day. Evening, we go to Exhibition and Ball at Pine Grove House.

September 10. Horton went to Brownsville to get a tooth extracted—he took two ladies with *him to hold his head, I suppose, and why not?*

People did not seem to worry about the stage robberies, and constantly traveled the toll roads between the towns. Business was as brisk as ever at the hotel.

A flock of sheep herded past fountain and water trough, viewed from the second floor of the hotel.

Lotta Crabtree. Courtesy Carl Mautz.

Chapter Eight
HIGH TIMES
1878-1881

Well, Lizzie, I suppose you were at Woodville, dancing your legs almost off, or limbs, I should say, to be more polite.

—ALICE MAY

JAMES KELLY OWNED Woodville for thirteen years—a remarkable feat considering the turmoil of the times. He had property in Honcut that required attention as well, and his health problems made it difficult for him to manage his affairs. Diary entries hint that he neglected the upkeep of Woodville House, and did not employ a person to clean up after the teams and livestock that constantly traveled through town. He grew weary of hotel-keeping and running the town, and talked of selling out.

John C. Falck was looking for a place to move his family away from the heavy snows and long winters of the high country. For many years he had operated the Buckeye Mine at Sawpit Flat above La Porte. Falck was born in Sweden and had gone to sea as a boy, sailing to many foreign ports and finally becoming a mate. When his ship came around the Horn to California and landed in San Francisco in 1854, he left for the Sierra gold country. He became part owner and superintendent of the Buckeye Mine and prospered. In 1856, he returned to Sweden and married his sweetheart, Sophia Hedstrom, whom he brought back to Sawpit Flat. Their son, Charles Lawrence Falck, was born in Gibsonville on August 14, 1868.

On October 5, 1878, Falck noted in his ledger that he sold his interest in the mine to a New York company, and the following day went to Woodville. Twogood describes the result:

October 6, Sunday, 1878. I find Mr. Falck here to see the Woodville House and Ranch—he contemplates buying it for a home and we pray that he may succeed. Weather lovely and warm.

October 7, Monday. Falck is to be the Proprietor of the Woodville House—the purchase is made. Kelly goes to Honcut.

October 9, Wednesday. Mr. Falck brings his family to their home. Kelly seems not satisfied and surprised at their coming.

October 10, Thursday. Today $1,500 was paid on the property and the contract made safe thereby. P.M. Falck returns to the mountains to settle up business preparatory to leaving. Is pleasant, though there are signs of a storm.

October 16, Wednesday. Mr. Falck came down—and a welcome guest he is to his wife and family. We think them all right.

October 21, Monday. The day on which Falck was to have had possession of the Woodville House, but he has been deprived of his rights. Eve. Kelly went below to settle the bargain.

October 24, 1878. Is rather windy. Several teams here. Mr. Falck left here for Sawpit Flat this morn. We are anxiously waiting for him to assume command of the big Brick.

October 26, Saturday. Is fine—wind northerly. P.M. Mr. Falck came down in advance of his household goods, brought by Jas. McMillen.

November 3, Sunday. Mr. Falck's children start out with new toys—velocipede, wagon and rocking horse.

November 7, Thursday. Mr. Falck is determined not to give up the Woodville House which he has fairly bought and partly paid for, though it is very evident that Kelly is trying to freeze him out.

November 11, Monday. Falck and Kelly had a difficulty, after which Kelly acknowledged he said what Falck said he did.

November 16, Saturday. Falck started below to see about business connected with the transfer of the Woodville property. Kelly is going below on Monday.

November 17, Sunday. Mrs. Falck's little girl is not well—the Dr. came to see her.

On November 20, 1878, Falck paid $4,000 in gold coin, the balance of the purchase price. The land is described as "a claim to 160 acres" in wheat, vineyards and orchards, the fully furnished and equipped Woodville House, dining room, kitchen, saloon and all the livestock. Besides the hotel, other buildings on the townsite included bath houses, barns, smithies, a store and houses.

November 20, Wednesday. I go to Clipper. The driver says that Falck is to take possession tomorrow (?). So might it be, say I.

November 21, 1878. Is the day we long have sang. Mr. Falck has peaceable possession of the Woodville property after all. We were all invited to dine at the Woodville House and we had a fine dinner.

November 22, Friday. Sidelinger and I took account of hay and other stock about the place Kelly has for sale.

November 23, Saturday. The Kellys are still at the Woodville House.

November 28. The Kellys are still here. Weather is threatening at times.

November 29, Friday. Weather is pleasant, but we look for foul weather soon. Kelly and his daughter Maggie started to the Honcut. Eve is fine.

November 30, 1878. Cloudy part of the time. I go to Lodge at Strawberry Valley. We initiate Miss Lizzie Sharrer and she is a Templar worth having, too.

December 1, Sunday. Kelly is in the neighborhood again, but it is hoped only temporarily.

It turned out that Kelly had purchased the land adjoining Woodville and wasn't planning to live on his Honcut property, but rather next door.

December 3, Tuesday. The Kelly house is going up, down near the old Barker House that used to be. Eve. Falck finished hauling manure and it looks fine in the dooryard. Everything looks improved.

December 4. Signs of rain in the near future. The Surprise Party for Falcks at Woodville has come and we have a nice time. All Strawberry, Clipper and Mt. Hope are present.

The Falcks were finally able to settle into Woodville, and since the freight business was thriving, Falck joined them with his own string of freight wagons and teams of mules and horses.

John C. Falck posed for a photographer in Sweden before he left for California.

WOODVILLE HOUSE. **JOHN.C.FALCK** PROPRIETOR. NORTH EAST TP. YUBA CO. CAL.

From left: Freight barn, ballroom, hotel (bath house, old Abbott House and wood house in rear), stage barn across road, tollhouse and gate at upper right. Orchards behind hotel, garden to the right. Mule team with freight wagons approaches water trough. Stagecoach nears Woodville, coming downhill toward the tollhouse. Lithograph by C. L. Smith, 1878.

My father, Gus Robinson worked for Falcks —he was a hosteler—took care of all the horses that hauled freight. Falck kept big teams and this was one of the places where the stages and drayers changed teams, so they had to have a lot of horses or mules here. Each teamster either bought grain and hay and stored it in their section of the loft in the barn, or paid extra for Falck to supply it. My father's job was to have another team harnessed up, and when the stages and freight wagons pulled in, unhitch the teams, and hook up the fresh team. Then take the first team into the barn to be brushed down, cooled off, watered and fed and put up in stalls. He had to be fast unless the stage or drayers came around noon or toward evening, then they had a little more time because the drivers and passengers had a meal at the hotel or stayed overnight.
—Elizabeth Merian

Falck wasted no time in planning more improvements in Woodville. In May of 1879, he began to build a large ballroom next to the hotel. He wanted to finish it by July and hold a grand ball on Independence Day. The hotel's old third-floor ballroom would be used for guests and for storage.

The peace of the small towns was disturbed by another robbery on June 21, 1879, when the down stage from La Porte to Oroville was robbed three miles from Forbestown. The express box and the U. S. mail were taken. Twogood wrote: "June 21, 1879. We hear of the robbing of the Oroville-Forbestown Stage."

The ball went ahead as planned, and people flocked to Woodville House. Twogood noted:

Annual 4th of July Dance at WOODLEAF
Saturday Night, July 3rd
Music by Six-piece Orchestra
Usual Good Supper at Midnight
Tickets, Including Supper—$2.50
There will also be DANCING SUNDAY, with the same Good Orchestra

Monday, June 30. The Birmingham family calls at our house and we have a pleasant chat. Johnnie East is trimming cake for the Ball.

Tuesday, July 1. We are preparing for the "Glorious Fourth". Two cows and their calves were taken from here, belonging to the Freemore Bros.

Fourth of July 1879. Is pleasant and people begin to collect at Woodville House for the Ball to take place this eve. Midnight everything is lovely.

Saturday, July 5. We had a gay and unusually pleasant time last eve.

Woodville became a popular site for balls and celebrations, and the Falcks were known for their hospitality. They served a midnight banquet when the revelers' energy waned, and at times there were as many as five hundred guests. In an era when recipes for fried chicken began, "First, catch a nice

Top: *Newspaper advertisement for the Fourth of July ball, published after the town's name was changed to Woodleaf.*
Bottom: *Woodville ballroom and hotel, 1896. Decorations for the Fourth of July celebration included swags of red, white and blue bunting and freshly cut evergreen trees placed along the buildings. More trees were set up inside, trimmed with small flags, paper rosettes and strings of bright red fire-crackers that were set off outdoors after dark. Guests line the upper veranda of the hotel. Andy Arbucco, with a hammer at left, "was the most marvelous dancer."*

young chicken, kill, pluck the feathers, clean and cut up," a dinner for five hundred people was an enormous job. The work couldn't be done too far in advance, since the ice house was too small to store much fresh meat. We can only guess how many people were needed to pluck chickens, peel potatoes, pick and string green beans, shell peas, bake bread, pies and cakes, churn butter, and grind coffee beans. Boys ran back and forth to feed the wood cookstoves and outdoor ovens, and men set up dozens of tables and benches. And who washed all those dishes when dinner was over? There was even more cooking ahead. In the late morning, guests enjoyed a huge breakfast, then headed for their carriages or stayed over a day or two in the hotel. The cost of a ticket to the ball, including dinner, ranged from $2.00 to $2.50.[1]

Clara G. Hayes, a vivacious young lady who lived in Howland Flat, loved to go to the balls.

It was a big thing to go to the ball at Woodville, and we always took the horses and wagons so more people could go along. We put on all our finery and drove for hours to get to Woodville. There was dancing and music and lots of good things to eat, and we stayed up all night; after breakfast in the morning, we started home again.

Falck had recently acquired a square rosewood pianoforte from an old friend in payment for a debt. When the friend sailed for New York, he promised Falck that he would repay him. The piano arrived months later, having been shipped around the Horn to San Francisco, then by steamship to Marysville and by freight wagon to Woodville. Musicians from Woodville and nearby towns provided music on this beautiful instrument, and on violin, melodeon, flute, cello and horns.

During the Falcks' years at the Buckeye Mine and La Porte, they had become acquainted with Jack Crabtree, a co-worker, who had a spirited red-haired daughter. Lotta Crabtree and Charles L. Falck became close friends, and shared happy memories of their childhood in the gold-mining camps. Lotta became the most highly paid actress in the world,

Top: *Ticket to the Fourth of July ball, printed in 1909.*
Below: *Lotta Crabtree in costume.*

playing in the capitals of Europe and England and in the large cities of the United States. When she returned for visits, the Falcks welcomed her with grand receptions at Woodville where she put on extravagant shows of songs, drama and dance. After one of her visits, she gave the Falcks a silk dress bought in Paris that she had worn in her shows. It is a treasured family heirloom.[2]

The 4th of July was always a grand celebration at Woodville. Hundreds of people traveled in for the fun. We had races, games, feasting, drinking

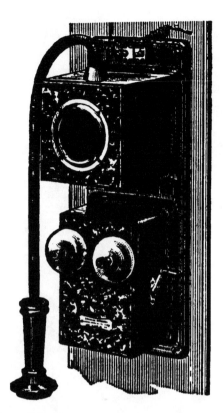

Telephone of the 1870s.

and dancing for days until the food ran out. When it was over, it meant the start of our main work season; cutting, drying and storing the wheat, picking and canning the fruit and vegetables, cider and wine-making, hauling freight by mule teams to the high mines and towns. This went on till the snow flew. We sometimes had to buy grain and hay from other ranches in order to have enough for the teams that stabled in the barn all during the year . . . from 150 to 200 at a time in the summer when travel was heavy on the pike.

—Helen Falck Dunning

The telephone had been invented only a short time before crews strung up the line into the area. Twogood wrote:

Tuesday, November 4, 1879. The telephone company men are getting near here with their posts. Eve. the telephone is in operation and questions are being asked and answered with people in Gibsonville, Howland Flat and La Porte.

Saturday, November 15. Shaw starts for Bangor. Osbeck's folks are getting settled in the house we just vacated. Lizzie Beckham went to Quincy.

It was costly to use the new invention—the charges were fifty cents for a conversation of ten words and three cents for each additional word. A telephone call in 1879 would have been quite restricted, if a typical conversation consisted of only ten words (five words per speaker), and an operator on the line counted each word that was spoken.

In spite of all the construction since Barker first settled in Woodville, its successive owners had possessed only a claim to the land. The Homestead Act of 1862 required that a person live on the property for five years in order to "patent" the claim, and as part of his agreement with Falck in selling Woodville, Kelly applied to the U.S. Land Office in Marysville for a patent on the 160 acres. In October of 1879 it was granted, and the land was at last private property.[3] But there was one problem—Kelly had a change of heart and did not want to hand over the promised document. Falck had to file suit with the Justice of the Peace in Strawberry Valley, forcing Kelly to deliver the patent. Falck was finally the legal owner.

Friday, December 5. Kelly and Falck have a lawsuit at Strawberry before Justice Youlen. We hear that Henry South died from the effects of a gun shot wound. Eve. we hear that he is still living and improving.

Monday, December 8. I salt my winter's beef. Shaw left with Falck for Brownsville.

Friday, December 12. Mr. Falck's dog is sick—probably poisoned by some enemy of Falck's.

Saturday, December 13. Nero, Mr. Falck's Newfoundland dog, is better.

—G. S. W. Twogood

The Falcks eventually made peace with their neighbor, Kelly. In fact, Falck was named guardian of Kelly's eldest son, Jeremiah, and both of Kelly's sons worked for Falck at Woodville for many years.[4]

Sunday, December 21. I get a few Christmas things for my folks at the Clipper store. I talk to E. A. Emmerson through the telephone—first experience in such witchery.

Monday, December 22. Snow 10 inches deep. I cut a tree out of the road. China Jim helped me. Birmingham took his daughter Lizzie Bird home to spend Christmas. The Adams family took a sleigh ride.

Saturday, December 27. This is the fiftieth anniversary of the birth of Gaylord Smith Wilsey Twogood.

Monday, December 29. Eve I got out my table to write and there was a surprise party. Came in sleighs from Strawberry Valley. After a good time, lunch, etc. they return by moonlight.

—G. S. W. Twogood

Timber fallers at work on a Douglas fir tree with axes and cross-cut saw.

Chapter Nine
GREEN GOLD
1878-1889

*Oh! What timber! These trees—these forests of trees …
monarchs to whom all worshipful men inevitably
lift their hats.*
—SAMUEL WILKESON, 1869

EASTERNERS HAD NEVER seen trees like these, soaring up to three hundred feet high and measuring twelve to fifteen feet across the base.[1] The early settlers in the Sierra Nevada Mountains brought saws with them, but they were only six or seven feet long, the largest sizes available at the time. While the manufacturers viewed the orders for eighteen-foot saws with skepticism, the Californians were drilling closely-spaced holes all around the tree trunks with long augers, and with axes and wedges, literally breaking the trees apart. The long saws eventually arrived, "misery whips" that barely eased the job of the woodsmen.

Besides lumber, men found a good market for shakes, shingles, posts, firewood, poles and wagon brake blocks among the growing population. Most of the country's resin and turpentine had been supplied by South Carolina, but when that state seceded from the Union prior to the Civil War, California rushed to fill the gap. Pine trees were tapped for resin and local distilleries made turpentine for the manufacturers of paint, wax, ink, glue and wood finishes. Bark for tanneries was gathered in the tan oak forests all around Woodville and shipped out by freight companies. Several tanneries operated nearby, one to the east near Oro Lewa and another to the west.

It was lumber that was in the highest demand, however, bringing such high prices that it became known as California's Green Gold.

Andrew Leach, an enterprising businessman, was rapidly accumulating land and mills during the early 1870s. In April of 1879, he bought 18.5 acres from Falck at Woodville, part of the south meadow where the Woodville Steam Sawmill was built. When Leach bought the Woodville store it seemed that the town might be divided into parcels at last.[2]

His timber land and mills eventually stretched from Strawberry Valley to Honcut and included the Clipper Mills, Deadwood, Cottage, Diamond Springs, Owl Gulch, Beanville, and Challenge mills. He owned more than 3,500 acres, plus the cutting rights to thousands more. The center of his company was located at Challenge, and in addition to the mill, included more than twenty buildings, among them a warehouse about 300 feet long, blacksmith shop, machine shop, a store and the Leach home. The logging trucks were built in the shop, and the axles, frames, U-bolts and metal-rimmed wooden wheels were manufactured on the site.

Leach had an unusual talent for management. Not only did he buy land and timber, oversee all the logging and mills, but he promoted and sold his

Logging with bull teams.

Leach's flume crosses the ravine beyond the Owl Gulch mill.
Right: *Andrew M. Leach, photographed at Woods'*
Photographic Art Gallery in Marysville in 1878.

own products as well.

Freighting the wood products to the valley by wagon was too slow and costly, however, and so an alternate method was needed to speed the lumber to market. A system of flumes carried the lumber from Leach's mills to the California Northern Railroad at Honcut, a distance of between fifty to eighty miles. The construction required about 135,000 board feet of lumber per mile, and the total cost for the flumes was between $200,000 and $320,000. They wound through the steep ravines, their trestles soaring 166 feet in the air in some places. Upkeep was a great expense; crews continually patrolled the system making repairs and clearing jams. Some portions were so steep that the water sped along at fifty miles an hour. The flumes were occasionally used to send crates of trout or venison packed in ice to friends and restaurants in the valley. Sometimes in an emergency a sick or injured person was sent flying down the flumes for medical treatment, but they surely had to be treated for shock once they arrived. There were always a few who would take the hair-raising trip on a dare, especially if they were drunk, but by the time they finished the trip, "they were soaking wet, shivering and stone-sober."

The flume drew its water from streams along the route, including Indian Creek as it passed by the Woodville Mill. Into the flume went 12 by 16 timbers up to 32 feet long, along with lumber of smaller dimensions, railroad ties, bundles of shakes, posts and poles.

Although most of the lumber was sent to the valley, local residents were steady customers. When Twogood built a new tollhouse at Woodville, he bought the lumber from Leach.

Tuesday, August 26. Birmingham is willing to furnish lumber, nails and paint for a new home I think of building for a Toll House.

Right: *Flume riders in V-shaped boat.*
Below: *The flume crew walked a narrow plank on the top of the flume, using picaroons to clear lumber jams.*

Friday, September 12. I order my lumber for a house from Leach whose wife has a baby 2 days old.

Monday, September 15. The first lumber for our new house came in.[3]

During 1884 Leach bought a locomotive and built a narrow gauge rail line from Challenge Mill to Beanville to haul logs and lumber. The line grew as the logging moved through the woods, and by 1889, it extended up Indian Creek.[4]

A. M. LEACH,

MANUFACTURER OF AND DEALER IN ALL KINDS OF

Lumber, Shingles, Shakes, &c

PROPRIETOR OF THE

Challenge, Cottage,

Diamond Springs, Clipper

and Deadwood Mills.

All orders promptly filled. Address, A. M. LEACH, Brownsville Postoffice, Yuba Co., Cal.

Left: *Advertisement for Leach's lumber company, 1879.*
Below: *The train crosses a trestle with a load of logs bound for the mill.*

On the fourth of July, Leach and his crews built seats and roofs for the flatcars, decorated them with flags and the people crowded aboard for a special holiday excursion.

Leach was the largest employer in the mountain area by now, and the economy centered around his operations. At Woodville, his mill produced around 40,000 board feet per day. The steady puffing of the sawmill and the wail of the steam whistle meant there was work and good pay. In the hotel, timber owners jostled with men selling the newest mill machinery as they waited for their steak dinners. Life was good, and they had money left over to jingle in their pockets.

A modern sawmill of 1879. The men use peavey hooks to move a log into position.

Black Bart, 1883. Courtesy Wells Fargo Bank.

Chapter Ten
BLACK BART
1875-1888

One would take him for a gentleman who had made money and was enjoying his fortune.
—HARRY MORSE

ON AUGUST 3, 1877, another stage was robbed, another Wells Fargo box taken. Over the past few years, there had been many holdups, but three of them appeared to have been the work of the same man: July 26, 1875, stage from Sonora to Milton; December 28, 1875, stage from San Juan to Marysville; June 2, 1876, stage from Roseburg to Yreka. In each of these robberies, the gunman was described as being of medium height wearing a long, linen duster that hid his clothing, a flour sack over his head with holes cut out for his eyes, with a deep voice and a surprisingly polite manner. In addition, each of the four express boxes had been chopped apart with a hatchet and the mail bags slashed open in exactly the same way. The news of this latest holdup brought the Wells Fargo agents to the site where the stage from Point Arena to Duncan's Mill had been robbed. They found not only the smashed treasure box, but a note written to them on one of their own waybills.[1]

> *I've labored long and hard for bread*
> *For honor and for riches*
> *But on my corns too long you've tred*
> *You fine haired sons of bitches.*
> —*BLACK BART, the Poet*

With this bit of doggerel, Black Bart became legend, and Wells Fargo at last had a name for the four-time robber. They plastered the poem on hundreds of wanted posters, sending them all over the state. Nearly a year later, on July 25, 1878, the Oroville-to-Quincy stage was robbed a mile above Berry Creek. At the scene of the robbery, Wells Fargo agents found the smashed and empty express box, and a second poem:

> *Here I lay me down to sleep*
> *To wait the coming morrow*
> *Perhaps success perhaps defeat*
> *And everlasting sorrow.*
> *Let come what will, I'll try it on,*
> *My condition can't be worse,*
> *But if there's money in the box,*
> *It's munny in my purse.*
> *Black Bart the Po8*
> —Wells Fargo Archives

The newspapers loved it. Reporters in San Francisco, Sacramento, and cities across the West spun out hundreds of stories, most of them fiction. The facts were quite enough to cause increasing embarrassment and irritation to Wells Fargo. Black Bart

Black Bart's first poem, left at the site of the robbery on August 3, 1877.

ARREST. STAGE ROBBER.

☞ These Circulars are for the use of Officers and Discreet Persons only. ☜

About one o'clock P. M. on the 3d of August, 1877, the down stage between Fort Ross and Russian River, was stopped by a man in disguise, who took from Wells, Fargo & Co.'s express box about $300 in coin and a check for $205 32, on Granger's Bank, San Francisco, in favor of Fisk Bros. On one of the way-bills left with the box, the robber wrote as follows :

I've labored long and hard for bread—
For honor and for riches—
But on my corns too long you've trod,
You fine haired sons of bitches.
BLACK BART, the Poet.

Driver, give my respects to our friend, the other driver; but I really had a notion to hang my old disguise hat on his weather eye.

Respectfully B. B.

It is believed that he went into the Town of Guerneville about daylight next morning.

About three o'clock P. M., July 25th, 1878, the down stage from Quincy, Plumas Co., to Oroville, Butte Co., was stopped by one masked man, and from Wells, Fargo & Co.'s box taken $379 coin, one diamond ring said to be worth $200, and one silver watch valued at $25. In the box, when found next day, was the following: [Fac simile.]

here I lay me down to sleep
to wait the coming morrow
perhaps success perhaps defeat
And everlasting sorrow
I've labored long and hard for bread
for honor and for riches
But on my corns too long you've tred
You fine haired sons of bitches
let come what will I'll try it on
My condition can't be worse
and if there's money in that Box
Tis munny in my purse

Black Bart
the Po 8

About eight o'clock A. M. of July 30th, 1878, the down stage from La Porte to Oroville was robbed by one man, who took from express box a package of gold specimens valued at $50, silver watch No. 716,996, P. S. Bartlett, maker.

It is certain the first two of these crimes were done by the same man, and there are good reasons to believe that he did the three.

There is a liberal reward offered by the State, and Wells, Fargo & Co. for the arrest and conviction of such offenders. For particulars, see Wells, Fargo & Co.'s "Standing Reward" Posters of July 1st 1876.

It will be seen from the above that this fellow is a character that would be remembered as a scribbler and something of a wit or wag, and would be likely to leave specimens of his handwriting on hotel registers and other public places.

If arrested, telegraph the undersigned at Sacramento. Any information thankfully received.

J. B. HUME, Special Officer Wells, Fargo & Co.

Left: *Wells Fargo distributed this circular to its agents and officers, describing several of Bart's robberies. Bart's second message included four lines from the first poem.* Below: *Poster from one of Bart's earlier robberies, where he gave the appearance of operating with a gang.*

REWARD!

Wells, Fargo & Co.,

Will Pay a Reward of $250 each for the Arrest and Conviction of the San Juan Express Robbers.

JOHN J. VALENTINE,
General Superintendent.

San Francisco, December 17th, 1875.

left no more notes, but the reporters and other writers were happy to provide a steady supply of bogus poems. The legend grew and the robberies continued:

July 30, 1878, La Porte stage
October 2, 1878, Cahto-Ukiah stage
October 3, 1878, Covelo-Ukiah stage

On June 21, 1879, the Oroville-La Porte stage was robbed by Black Bart three miles below Forbestown, and the express box and the U.S. mail were taken. Later, passengers on the Oroville-La Porte stage nervously watched every bend in the road, but Black Bart moved to another area of California, and the tension eased.

October 25, 1879, Roseburg-Redding stage
October 27, 1879, Alturas-Redding stage
July 22, 1880, Point Arenas-Duncan's Mills stage
September 1, 1880, Weaverville-Redding stage
September 16, 1880, Roseburg-Yreka stage
November 20, 1880, Redding-Roseburg stage
August 31, 1881, Roseburg-Yreka stage
October 8, 1881, Yreka-Redding stage
October 11, 1881, Lakeview-Redding stage

On December 15, 1881, Black Bart robbed the

Downieville-to-Marysville stage four miles from Dobbins Ranch. He was back again, and Wells Fargo agents prowled the countryside. He shifted his operations to another area, then returned, seemingly without any pattern for the weary detectives to follow.

December 27, 1881, North San Juan-Smartsville stage, on South Fork of Yuba River

January 26, 1882, Ukiah-Cloverdale stage

June 14, 1882, Little Lake-Ukiah stage

When the stage left La Porte bound for Oroville on July 13, 1882, it was carrying $18,000 in gold bullion, and Wells Fargo had assigned George Hackett, one of their best messengers, to guard the shipment. About fifteen miles above Woodville, Black Bart stepped out in front of the stage and pointed his shotgun at the messenger. The driver, Hank Helm, described what happened next:

As soon as Hackett could get his gun ready, he fired. The gun was loaded with buckshot. The robber then made a motion as if to shoot, but didn't seem able to get his gun to his shoulder. He then ran around to the other side of the leader [horse] and I yelled to Hackett, 'sock it to him.' Hackett then fired . . . the contents of his second barrel. The robber then took to his heels . . . he ran down the hill, straight away from the road. We picked up the robber's hat on the road. It was a soft hat, of black felt, very old and weather-beaten and full of ragged rents. It had four fresh buckshot holes in it, with hair sticking to some of them. The man's hair was light in color, streaked with gray. As he ran down the hill he tore off his mask, and I noticed that he had a bald spot on the top of his head. The whole thing happened in half a minute.

Marysville-La Porte stage in front of the hotel. Photograph by Louis Stellman.

Above: *Painting of Bart robbing a stage, showing the long linen duster he wore, and the flour sack over his head.*
Above right: *Gold ingot cast by Wells Fargo in 1854 from nuggets and gold dust shipped in from miners. It weighed sixteen ounces and was worth $325 at the time.*
Right: *The strongbox that carried the gold was about two feet long, one foot high and one foot deep.*

Helm drove the stage to Forbestown where Hackett changed stages and took the treasure box to Oroville. With Frank Morse driving, they had traveled about seven miles when a masked robber tried to climb aboard the stage from the back. Hackett fired his gun at the same time as the robber, and a bullet grazed Hackett's face; the robber escaped. When Hackett recovered from his wound, Wells Fargo rewarded him with a gold watch for his

remarkable achievement—the only messenger to foil two robberies in one day. Hackett testified that this was not the same man who had attempted the robbery earlier in the day, but years later when the road department put up a monument at the spot, they mistakenly declared it was the scene of one of Black Bart's holdups.[2]

After a second robbery attempt in one day, the people were in an uproar. Gus Robinson, a nephew of the Falcks, said there had been at least one calm person at Woodville, that nice gentleman from San Francisco:

> Last night we had dinner at the Woodville House and sat around talking about the stage that was nearly robbed just up the road. Quite a few guests were at the House, and everybody was nervous, but Mr. Bolton the mining speculator from San Francisco said he thought we were unnecessarily worried. He retired from our conversation early as he was not feeling well.
> —August Robinson, July 14, 1882[3]

Rumors spread like the wind—Black Bart had stayed at a hotel in Marysville; he stopped for breakfast at the Adams' house at Oro Lewa; he was seen hiding out in a neighbor's barn; he escaped through an old Chinese tunnel in Oroville. The newspaper reports spun out fantastic tales, and no one knew what to believe. One thing was certain: Black Bart continued his crime spree.

September 17, 1882, Yreka-Redding stage
November 24, 1882, Lakeport-Cloverdale stage
April 12, 1883, Lakeport-Cloverdale stage
June 23, 1883, Jackson-Ione City stage
November 3, 1883, Sonora-Milton stage

When agents searched the site of the Sonora-to-Milton stage near Copperopolis, they found, among other things, a white silk crepe handkerchief with a faint imprint of a laundry mark on the edge. James B. Hume had spent eight years chasing Black Bart, and now, armed with the laundry mark, FX07, he checked the laundries in dozens of cities until he found one in San Francisco that used the mark. "I know Mr. Bolton well," said the shop owner. "He is in the city now; just arrived from his mine two days ago . . . Why, here comes the very man now." Detective Harry Morse recalled,

> I knew at once from the description of the fellow that this was Black Bart. He was elegantly dressed and came sauntering along swinging his cane. He wore a natty derby hat, a diamond pin, a large diamond ring and a heavy gold watch and chain. He was about five feet eight inches tall, straight as an arrow, with fine broad shoulders, with deep sunken blue eyes, high cheek bones and a handsome gray mustache and imperial. One would take him for a gentleman who had made money and was enjoying his fortune.

Hume politely questioned Mr. Bolton while officers searched his rooms at the Webb House. They found clothing with the FX07 laundry mark, the long linen duster he wore during robberies, and a bible inscribed to Charles E. Boles from his wife, dated 1865.

Record of Bart's arrest for highway robbery in San Andreas, Calaveras County.

BLACK BART
The Notorious Stage Robber at last Captured.
PROOF AS TO HIS IDENTITY
TRUE NAME CHARLES BOLES
—San Francisco Examiner,
November 14, 1883

Listed in the newspaper article were his aliases, among them, Charles Bolton. His photograph and description left no doubt that Mr. Boles and Mr. Bolton were the same man, and that Gus Robinson had dined with Black Bart after the attempted robbery of the La Porte-to-Oroville Stage. As he had just had his hat shot off, it was no wonder he "retired early, as he wasn't feeling well."

The shocking news was quick to reach the Sierras. His friends were stunned. Mrs. Falck studied the hotel register, where C. E. Bolton had signed his name, and grieved, "He was the only real gentleman ever to stay in the hotel." Mary, known as the "Belle of Woodville," had been courted by Charles during the past eight years. She was heartbroken and could scarcely believe the reports.

Charles Boles confessed to the last robbery, and agreed to return the treasure remaining—he had spent about $300 on a custom-made suit of Harris tweed, new derby hat, and traveling expenses. Boles led the agents to the stash of gold in a hollow log, not far from the hold-up site. He continued to insist that he was not Black Bart, but pleaded guilty to one robbery, and Judge C. V. Gottschalk sentenced him to six years in San Quentin. Newspapers across the country headlined the news of the "gentleman bandit." Mrs. Boles, who was living in Hannibal, Missouri, with one of their married daughters, recognized the descriptions of her husband, who she

Charles Boles, the infamous Black Bart, and his wife, Mary Elizabeth Boles.
Courtesy Wells Fargo Bank, left, and Marc C. Reed Collection, right.

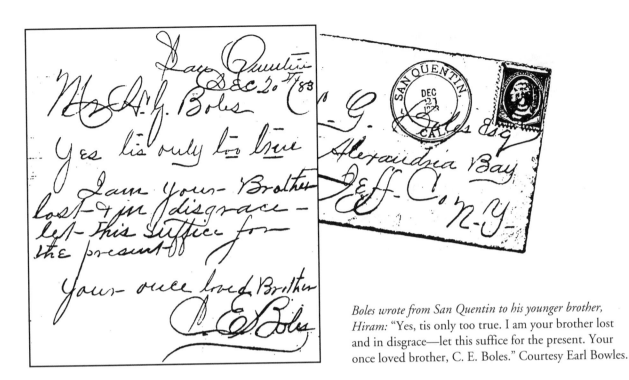

Boles wrote from San Quentin to his younger brother, Hiram: "Yes, tis only too true. I am your brother lost and in disgrace—let this suffice for the present. Your once loved brother, C. E. Boles." *Courtesy Earl Bowles.*

thought was dead. In 1865, he had left his family for the gold fields, promising to send for them. He wrote frequent letters to them from the Montana Territory, sometimes four a week. When his letters suddenly stopped, his wife presumed he had met with misfortune and had been killed. She brought up the children alone, eking out a living as a seamstress while he lived as a wealthy "gentleman." Throughout his time in prison, she wrote to him, and he responded with affectionate letters. He was released on January 21, 1888, but he never returned to her and their children.

Mrs. Sophia Falck, too, received a letter from Boles, which became a treasured family keepsake:

> *Charles Boles wrote a letter to mother, apologizing for deceiving her, and for any embarrassment he might have caused the family, and for the notoriety he had brought to the Woodville Hotel.[4]*
> —Charles Falck

Charles Boles was born in England in 1829, and a year later his family came to America where he grew up. He spent three years in California during the Gold Rush, then returned home and married.

During the Civil War, he served three years in the Union Army as a first sergeant, Company B, 116th Illinois Infantry. He was with General Sherman's march through Georgia, where he was wounded and honorably discharged June 7, 1865.

No one knows why he became a criminal. In engineering the robberies, Boles poked black-painted broomsticks over rocks to give the impression of gun barrels pointed at the driver by a gang of thieves. Although he carried a gun, he never fired a shot, and it was later discovered that the gun had never been loaded. Sometimes his boots were wrapped in old sacks to obscure his footprints. Always the gentleman to the stagecoach passengers, especially the ladies, Boles never robbed their valuables, but concentrated on the Wells Fargo box.

Between robberies, Boles posed as a mining engineer and speculator during those eight years. As C. E. Bolton, a San Francisco resident, he was highly respected and a friend of many prominent citizens. He dined often at the popular New York Bakery, where mining company executives and law enforcement men often met; in fact, Boles was acquainted with many of them. The stylishly dressed Charles did not smoke or drink and traveled in the best of company; he was considered a fascinating and witty

Note from "Mary" to "Charley," found in the Woodville Hotel: "Charley, drop one pearl in memory's casket, for your friend, Mary E. Hall, Woodville, May 24, 1883."

man of great charm. His arrest and conviction revealed a totally different character: a roadside robber, thief and liar who had deserted his wife and children. He may have been a bigamist, as well.

After his release, Wells Fargo agents followed Boles' every move as he used one alias after another—Spaulding, Barlowe, Barnes, Moore. Suddenly, he managed to elude them, and dropped completely out of sight. According to his nephew, he traveled by night heavily disguised to Woodville to meet Mary Vollmer, who was then in her early thirties. Boles' nephew claims that Charles and Mary made their way secretly to Harrisburg, Pennsylvania, and were married, living out their lives in quiet obscurity.

Countless stories have been told of Black Bart's final years, the majority of which are sheer fantasy. Most of the poems supposedly written by him have proved to be fakes. Only twelve letters have been authenticated. The story about Mary is included here because of several pieces of information that suggest it may be worth consideration. The story of the "Belle of Woodville" (or Woodleaf) was told by John and Sophia Falck, Charles and Agnes Falck, and, later, by the cooks at Woodleaf in the 1940s. The legend would not seem worth recalling by itself, but at least one historian, R. E. Bosshard, inter-

viewed Mary Vollmer during the 1930s, and she confirmed the story. Two historians, William Collins and Bruce Levene, traced Mary Vollmer, and found that she was listed in the Harrisburg, Pennsylvania, city directories in the 1880s and 1890s, and that she died January 23, 1940.

Boles wrote a third poem while he was in San Quentin, for a little girl named Nellie Owen. The Owen family lived at the Webb House in San Francisco and knew Mr. Bolton, who also lived there. Nellie Owen described him as "a quiet, kindly gentleman . . . who was away at times on business connected with his mining interests." Nellie's father, Samuel Owen, a naval architect, took her with him when he visited Boles in San Quentin. In the poem, the letters at the beginning of each line spell "Nellie."

Never, oh never shall I forget
Engraved in my heart is your image, sweet pet
Like the sunbeams and dewdrops pure sparkling
and bright
Like the bright stars of heaven shedding forth
their soft light
In memory's casket you never shall lie
Ever, forever, dear Nellie goodbye.
—San Quentin, circa 1883-88

In 1970, an engraved card was found beneath the wallcovering in one of the rooms favored by Bolton in the Woodleaf hotel. The card reads, "Charley, Drop one pearl in memory's casket for your friend, Mary E. Hall, Woodville, May 24, 1883." Does the name "Charley" refer to Charles Boles? Did "Mary E. Hall" also use the name of Mary Vollmer? There is no proof, but Levene and Collins state that "the appearance of 'in memory's casket,' in two poems . . . is almost beyond the range of probability." The fact remains, however, that no one has proved what became of Charles Boles after his release from San Quentin. In spite of many rewards offered for a final answer, Black Bart's story ended in mystery.[5]

Black Bart was not the only famous guest at the Woodville House during those times. Some years after the end of the Civil War, President Ulysses S. Grant toured the West, staying in many towns in the Gold Rush area, and he was an honored guest at Woodville House. Today, it is difficult to realize that the tremendous wealth of the north Sierra could justify a visit by the President, but the gold pouring into the treasury from the California hills was of vital importance to the country, particularly after the Civil War drained its resources and left it heavily in debt. President Grant may have known of the secession of Rough and Ready, and wished to tour the mines and towns in the area to strengthen their loyalties. He may also have been motivated by his ambition to be nominated for another term. In addition, some of his wife's relatives lived nearby, and the President may have found it equally important to visit his in-laws.[6]

Stagecoach on mountain road; by Charles C. Nahl.

Woodville, 1896. John C. Falck, —, Laurence Wooley, —, Sophia Falck, entertainer, —.
Charles L. Falck stands on the second floor veranda; to his left, the image of his first wife is scratched out.

Chapter Eleven
THE END OF DREAMS
1883-1899

The snow was twelve feet on the level and twenty feet in drifts . . . . We hadn't expected this from California!
—MAUDE GILBERT HILL

PROPERTY PRICES were low in 1883. The Central Pacific Railroad offered surplus land for sale, and the forty acres on the north side of Woodville became available. Falck paid $70 in gold coin for the parcel, which added a beautiful piece of land to Woodville. While the parcel had cost only $1.75 an acre, it cost $3 to record the deed.[1]

Land values fell even further in the years ahead. For more than thirty years the mountains had been washed away by hydraulic mining, which filled the streams and rivers with silt and smothered the valley ranches with mud and debris. Ships were finding it increasingly difficult to navigate the rivers. The courts became battlegrounds as lawsuits were brought to halt hydraulic mining. Open-pit, tunnel and quartz mines were not affected, since they were less destructive. Hydraulic mining had devastating consequences, but it was a thousand times more profitable than any other mining technique, and gold, as always, had a powerful effect. Merchants, bankers and miners were all swayed by it. In 1884, the Anti-Debris Act was passed; hydraulic mining slowed, but the battle continued before it was finally stopped.[2] At last there was relief for the valley people, but not since the Gold Rush had so great a shock hit the high Sierras.

Thousands of men lost their jobs. They laid down their tools and walked away from their sluices and monitors. They left their houses, barns and gardens as they stood, and if they had no wagon, they left the furnishings inside.[3] Celluloid collars lay on the dressers, quilted coverings on the beds; paper dolls were arranged for play, the dishes and silver stored neatly in the sideboards, Persian rugs on the floor. Families crowded onto buggies and stages and headed down the pass. Through Strawberry Valley, Clipper Mills and Woodville, wagons came driven by men looking for work and a home for their families. A great many scattered across the state to start a new life.

Shortly after the birth of her son John in 1870, Nellie Kennedy's husband died and she married Samuel Johnson, a miner in the Nelson Point area. The Johnsons had lived in La Porte, Gibsonville and Nelson Point for a number of years. During this difficult time, these Maidu moved back to Pakan'yani with their son John and daughter Elizabeth and their families.

Some of the men found work in Andrew Leach's mills and logging operations, the largest independently-owned lumber business of the time, as well as the longest lived. His mills, flumes and factories were in production for fifteen years, while the giant corporations had only managed to stay afloat from two to six years. In October of 1887, however, the first of a series of disasters befell the Leach empire. The Challenge Mill burned with a loss of over a half million board feet of lumber, and then the planing mill and box factory at Moore's Station near Honcut went up in flames. A few weeks later, Woodville Steam Sawmill was completely destroyed by fire.

The winter of 1889-90 brought heavy snows to the Sierra. At Woodville, it was twelve feet on the level, and twenty feet in drifts. Great sections of the Leach Company flumes collapsed into the canyons under the tremendous weight. The combined loss from fire and snow was devastating. Leach planned to rebuild the Woodville and Challenge mills, but the country was hit by a severe depression in 1893, and his lumber empire disintegrated. Leach sold off pieces of land or traded acreage to his creditors while trying to reorganize and rebuild. Because of the depression, however, no money was available to finance the reconstruction, and by the spring of 1890 more than forty-five suits had been filed in the courts by workers and creditors. Among them was George Hill, former owner of Barker House, who had given up on mining and worked at one of the mills. Leach gave George a number of acres near Challenge in payment for his wages. Thirty men made similar arrangements for land, although some accepted other goods—Mr. Adams of Oro Lewa received a white horse named Flora. The eighteen and a half acres at Woodville, now black with the ashes of the Woodville Steam Sawmill, eventually reverted to government ownership, and are now part of the U.S. Forest Service lands.[4]

Maude Gilbert Hill tells of her experiences as a child living near Woodville, and the winter of 1889:

My father took up a homestead and we reveled in all 160 acres of this virgin timber land and the beauty surrounding the small town of Woodville.[5] He was a violinist of considerable talent. When an accident caused the partial loss of the use of one arm, he held his cherished violin between his knees and played the instrument backward. Often in the long evenings he played the violin or played games with us children.

Our school, the Empire Hill District, was near our house . . . we nearly always went home for lunch. The school had a spring and a patch of honeysuckle and huckleberries and we picked the berries so mother could make pies.

Our first winter on our Woodville homestead in 1889 surprised us with its intensity and cold. The snow was twelve feet on the level and twenty feet deep in drifts. We had to dig tunnels to the door and windows for light and to get in and out. Every time a snowslide fell from the roof in the night, mother jumped, fearful that the tree was

Inside the Clipper Mills school; Miss Loveless, teacher.

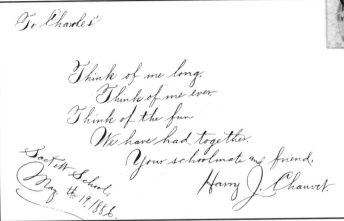

Page from Charles Falck's autograph album with a note from a classmate at Sackett's Academy in 1881, and calling cards of Charles, Arthur and Hilma Falck, 1884.

falling on the house. Men with block and tackle removed the oaks from the hovering positions, the weight of the snow having toppled many of them. We hadn't expected this from California!

When the men had finished their work, mother served them coffee, homemade bread, roast pork, vegetables, pumpkin pie, and sweet cider.

At this time I came to know sadness never before encountered. Typhoid fever was rampant, and my uncle Oliver Hankins who stayed with us was the first to succumb. Later my father became ill, and his was a lengthy illness. We had no money. From his sick-bed my father made arrangements to mortgage the homestead in order to pay the nurse who came to stay and the doctor who came from Forbestown once a week. After six weeks of acute illness, my father died, as beloved as any father could be.

The man who loaned us money tore up the mortgage knowing that without father there was no chance of repayment. I saw many acts of kindness and generosity during that time. These people knew my father; they knew that he would have done likewise for them.

Also in 1889, after years away at school, Charles Falck came home to help his parents manage the businesses at Woodville. He had attended Sacketts Academy in Oakland, then Pacific Business College in San Francisco, graduating in 1886. In addition to his business aptitude, Charles had a compassionate heart. Records in the county archives show that on many occasions he gave food, clothing, shoes and tools from the store to families whose homes had burned or who had lost their providers through accident or death.

Charles had witnessed grieving families seeking lumber for the painful task of building coffins. His own family knew grief, for his little brother, Arthur, had died at the age of three in 1885. Charles opened the Coffin House southwest of the store and stage barn, ordering coffins from San Francisco. He kept a stock of French velvet, silk and satin fittings so that each coffin could be finished to order. To complete the service, he bought a fine hearse carriage that could be hired for funerals.

As the economy slowed, so did the freight busi-

ness, and by 1890, Charles had sold all the teams and freight wagons, keeping only two horses and two cows. The value of Woodville House that year was calculated at $2,000, his father's gold watch at $100, his mother Sophia's sewing machine at $20, and the land at about $1.50 an acre.[6] The sewing machine was a valuable asset not only to the Falcks, but to the Maidu, and Sophia traded it for a selection of Nellie's beautiful baskets. Fine wool

Charles L. Falck, H. F. Hogan studio, Oroville.

Left: *Baskets made by Nellie Johnson (Tasu'mili) and traded to the Falcks. The large tray at the back was used to separate grain from chaff; the bowl at left has an unusual leaf design; symbols for flying geese decorate the larger bowl at right. The small bowl at the center was used to serve food; at the front, the bowl's design symbolizes hunting. The V-shaped emblems are birds; the arrows pointing up indicate that the hunter hit a bird with every other arrow shot. Below: A sewing machine of similar design was traded for baskets.*

clothing, blankets, and tools were also exchanged for a great variety of the handwoven baskets until Sophia had a large collection.[7] The Falck children and grandchildren were allowed to play with the baskets in the evenings, as stories were told of Tasu'mili, Ya'lo and his wife living in the ancient village of Pakan'yani.

In a cabin by the spring Nellie lived with her son, John Kennedy, his wife, Sarah, and their children. Partly in the old world and partly in the new, Nellie was sixty-three years old in 1890, and honored as one of the elders of her tribe. During the day, the grandchildren went to the Empire Hill School, learned to read and write, and heard stories about other civilizations. The men worked for merchants and ranchers while the women did housework and sold their baskets. In the fall they trekked to the top of the hill carrying baskets, fur ornaments and jewelry, and upon a signal from the elders, began the burning in honor of those who had died in years

Teams of horses and mules line up in front of the Woodville Hotel with freight and hay wagons. The first in line has two wagons in tandem. Near the ballroom, more freight wagons wait to be unloaded and to have fresh teams put in harness.

past. One year, the sewing machine was among the things of value that was burned. The family still made trips to Pomingo and La Porte to gather plants, acorns and material for baskets, camping far back in the meadows away from the busy roads.

The increasing publicity of the Indians' plight, combined with low land values, at last moved the federal government to purchase several hundred acres of land near Feather Falls. The Mooretown Rancheria was established, and it was returned to the Maidu in 1894. Nellie and her family, however, remained at Woodville and Strawberry Valley.

Gradually, the Woodville area recovered from the depression, and freighting increased until by 1897 there were six to eight teams in town every night. Charles Falck invested in wagons and teams and

went back into the business. When the Woodleaf Store came up for sale, he bought it back for $35.[8]

In 1898 the Klondike Gold Rush swept thousands from the country and into the frozen land of the Yukon Territory in northwest Canada. Again there was a drop in population, but a much smaller one. Perhaps the lure of gold was not so great to those who knew the costs of pursuing it.

With forty-six people living at Woodville, Charles Falck petitioned the U.S. government for a post office, a convenience the town had lacked for forty years. Since there was by now another Woodville in California with a U.S. post office (in Tulare County), the town needed a new name. Falck suggested "Woodleaf," and as a second choice, "Falck." The people waited for the news, ready with their sign boards and paint to change the town's name. Would it be Falck or Woodleaf? The letter came at last, establishing a post office on July 6, 1898. Charles Falck was appointed postmaster, and Woodleaf was the new name of the town.

In addition to his many business pursuits, Charles was trustee and clerk of the Empire School Board. Empire School was located above Woodleaf and Oro Lewa in the little town of Empire Hill, and the children in Woodleaf attended classes there. The board hired a new teacher in 1899, and Agnes Riker moved into one of the cottages at Woodleaf.[9] She was five feet five inches tall, bright and high-spirited. Charles Falck, at age thirty-one, was the town's most eligible bachelor, and he lost no time during the last year of the century. After a brief courtship, they were married on April 5 in San Francisco. Agnes Falck began a new life at Woodleaf, and the school board was left to find another teacher.

It was the end of some dreams, but for others, it was only the beginning.

Agnes Falck, photographed as a young woman.
M. E. Phares studio, Oroville.

Waiting for the mail at the Woodleaf Store.

Chapter Twelve
A NEW CENTURY
1900-1919

*Woodleaf was a hangout for a lot of characters …
if anything was going to happen, it usually happened
at Woodleaf.*
—JACK DUNNING

SOME PREDICTED the end of the world when 1900 neared; others said it was the beginning of a grand new day for humanity. A few commented sourly that the next century actually did not begin until 1901. Nevertheless, 1900 was greeted with hope for better times and with many parties; of course, there was one at Woodleaf. This party was different because young Mrs. Falck was there to help with the dinner for five hundred guests. Agnes had interests beyond frying chicken, however. In 1911, while suffragettes in other states were thrown in jail for demonstrating, Yuba County passed a ballot issue granting women the vote in local elections. It would be eight more years before all women in the United States won the right to take part in national elections. Agnes drove her carriage to Strawberry Valley and signed the register for 1912, along with seven other women. The Falck men had always been "Republicans and proud of it," and wives were expected to vote in the same political party as their husbands. Agnes registered as a Democrat.

The new century also brought loss to the Falcks when the patriarch of the family died. Twogood continued to chronicle the changing times.

October 8. Sunshine this morn. Seven teams left here this morning, including Falck's. Minstrel Show at Clipper Mills tonight.

November 25. Rain falls lively from early morn till noon. Wife and I commence making preparations to move to our home in Brownsville.[1]

December 5. We hear that Mr. John C. Falck died at 10 a.m. yesterday. Weather rainy and windy.

December 27, 1901. This is the 73rd anniversary of my birthday. I cannot realize that I am so aged. I read and write without spectacles in the day time, and I'm straight. A present of a pair of slippers came to me through the mail. We hear of the birth of a son to the wife of J. H. McCrank. Wind north.

Twogood and Falck were lured to the Sierra by gold, as were so many others, but they stayed to make their homes, raise families and live out their lives. The qualities of life that held them began to draw the attention of city dwellers. The cool mountains and quiet towns were enticing to those who wished to escape a frenetic lifestyle, and prices for lodging were low. At first only a few vacationers came with their families for the summer; then the pace picked up, as people traveled from San Francisco, Oakland, Berkeley and southern California. It was the beginning of a new industry, noted by the newspapers of Oroville and Marysville, which ran columns for each mountain town. Even Woodleaf had its own column.

WOODLEAF

Quite a number of people from Alameda and San Francisco are spending their summer in this vicinity. Both the hotel at Clipper and Woodleaf are filled with summer tourists.

Mr. Roseberry furnishes us some lovely music on the piano dulcimer.
—Marysville Daily Appeal, June-July, 1904

Mrs. T. A. Crellon and her five daughters left

here last Saturday in a surrey from Fry brothers livery stable in Forbestown en route to Oakland.

Mrs. J. M. Beck took the stage for Marysville last Saturday morning en route to her home in Pasadena.

Professor Charles Gullick came down from the residence of G. W. Shearer with his friend, Mr. Marks, who took the stage with Austin Jones en route to his home in Oakland last Thursday.
—Butte Record, July 15, 1904

Twogood writes:

1904, May 20. This is a fine morning. P.M. I took Lizzie and baby Lawrence up to Adam's. They will be at the Masquerade Ball tomorrow night at Falck's.[2]

August 1. Is warm. There are three drummers [traveling salesmen] here for the night.

November 10. We get news of a perfect landslide for everybody's favorite, Theodore Roosevelt for President of these United States. California Republicans did themselves proud on ElectionDay.

1905, April 25. I ride to Coppock's and Moore's place returning via Ruff's where I have dinner and a fine treat to gramophone music.[3]

June 1, 1905. Dan Boland had a runaway from Mt. Hope to the top of the hill near what is called "Cape Horn" on the Forbestown road. Looks like rain.

June 17. Is pleasant again. Carmichael's last band of stock, cattle, horses, mules and sheep arrive about 6:40 having been driven from the White House this morning.

August 17. Brown's sheep are here—1,200 he says.

Brownsville Meat Market made deliveries to homes and stores throughout the area, and also did the butchering for people at their ranches. Henry Kloss in wagon, J. L. Campbell on ground. Photograph by Peterson-Bean.

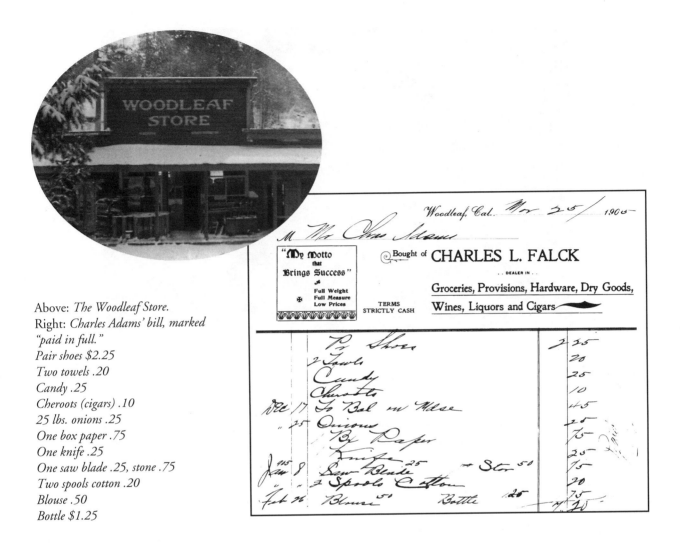

Above: *The Woodleaf Store.*
Right: *Charles Adams' bill, marked "paid in full."*
Pair shoes $2.25
Two towels .20
Candy .25
Cheroots (cigars) .10
25 lbs. onions .25
One box paper .75
One knife .25
One saw blade .25, stone .75
Two spools cotton .20
Blouse .50
Bottle $1.25

Adams' diaries reveal another view of life:

> *April 18, 1906. Fair. Worked in the Tunnel all day. Earthquake at 4:45 San Francisco nearly destroyed.*
> *May 6, 1906. Tottie, Bud and I went to Woodville and got two pair of shoes for Bud. Paid Charles Falck all up to date $26.95.*
> *May 29, 1906. Went up to Barton Hill and got my gum boots and some tools and went prospecting down on Slapjack. Keith brought Will Schultz a load of freight and paid him $12.00 on my account.*
> *July 4, 1906. Went to the Celebration at Woodleaf. Took charge of the Turkey Shoot.*

In 1906, Twogood noted:

> *June 4, 1906. I spend business hours of the forenoon in the Supervisors' Office. They established rates of toll on Marysville and La Porte Turnpike for Birmingham.*

As early as 1860, there were widespread complaints about the costs of traveling the toll roads, and at that time, a one-way trip from Marysville to La Porte cost $14 in tolls. Toward the end of the century, Yuba County gradually bought the privately owned turnpikes, building a network of public roads. In 1906, the Board of Supervisors purchased the eight-mile road between Woodleaf and

The Binet family of Clipper Mills out for a drive in their new automobile.

Strawberry Valley from Mr. Birmingham for $600. The gates were taken down, Twogood left his post as tollkeeper, and one of the oldest roads in the county was opened for free travel.[4] Free, that is, except for the new taxes levied by the county.

From his store in Brownsville, Twogood noted something new on the old road:

> *June 19, 1907. The man went down with the Automobile today.*

The Binet family of Clipper Mills was considered very daring to buy one of those new-fangled machines. The vehicles weren't appreciated by everyone—they were noisy, smelly, raised a lot of dust and had all kinds of mechanical problems that couldn't be solved with a bucket of oats and a few choice words.

The gold mine at Woodleaf was equally noisy with its steam engines and dynamite. The mine was located on the Kelly property, which Antonio Arbucco and a partner from Oregon, Joseph Supple, bought from Eli Harter and began operating in 1908. They called it the Beik Supple Mine, but it was more commonly known as Mt. de Oro Mine.

They installed a stamp mill in 1927 to pound the gold-bearing quartz into pulp, and the roar and rumble could be heard from miles away. When the costs finally became too high for the gold recovered, they closed it down.[5]

> *A couple of high-class fellows from the East leased the old mine and started it up again. They got enough out to make one ingot and sold it to the old Decker and Jewett Bank in Marysville for about $700. The ingot turned out to be almost fifty percent brass when it was tested, because the chemicals and acids used in processing the gold had been too strong and had dissolved the insides of the brass valves of the equipment. The "operators," though, had skipped the country.*
> —Jack Dunning

Another noisy industry arrived in 1910, when Butte County Pine and Hardwood Lumber Company bought wood-burning steam engines, intending to haul freight, lumber and logs from their mill near Woodleaf to Oroville. People came to watch the huge, fire-belching engines pass by, worrying that the whole area would be set ablaze.

Petitions and letters flooded the county, and the County Board of Supervisors demanded that the engines be converted to oil. Mr. Dickey, the manager, replied that they were completely safe, and that engines were operating in other areas without problems. By using wood, he explained,

> *It would give employment to many people up along the road cutting wood off their own land. . . . We are paying them $5 per cord . . . leaving*

the money in Butte county instead of paying it out down here to the Standard Oil Company.
—Oroville Mercury

The Board of Supervisors persisted, and Dickey at last gave in and converted the engines. He added a night service between Oroville and Woodleaf to keep up with the demand for lumber. Local mule freighting companies were ready to abandon the route because of the competition. Adams was

Steam engine and crew on the way to pick up a load of lumber. Photograph by Peterson.

TRACTION TRAINS HERE
FOR WOODLEAF ROUTE

BUTTE PINE AND HARDWOOD COMPANY WILL START
ITS MILL AND FREIGHT SERVICE
BY MAY FIRST

MAY ENJOIN TRACTION
ENGINES FOR FEAR FIRE

Residents along the line of the
ite of the traction engine service
ated between this city and
hear over the country road have
protest to the board of su
and the Forestry Servic
he company operating its
th wood as fuel. It was

reported at the meeting of the
ber of commerce
Secretary N
ere

TRACTION ENGINE
TO USE OIL

BIG BUSINESS DEVELOPED BY
LINE OF WOODLEAF LUM-
BER CONCERN

TRACTION
ENGINE A
FAILURE

Headlines from the Oroville-Mercury *newspaper tell the story of Mr. Dickey and his traction engines.*

among those cutting logs for the new company:

> *April 20, 1910, Wednesday. Fair. George, Lloyd and I commenced cutting logs for the Butte Pine and Hardwood Company.*
>
> *May 20, Friday. Fair. Traction Engine took our shakes away this morning. Planted garden and got water on it in forenoon. Sawed logs p.m.*

On May 27, the Oroville Mercury noted:

> *BUTTE COUNTY PINE AND HARD-WOOD LUMBER COMPANY TAKES OUT 21 TONS*
>
> *Changed over to oil burners the traction engines of the Butte County Pine and Hardwood Lumber Company hauled a train of cars carrying 21 tons of freight for Woodleaf merchants this morning. The company has 21,000 feet of lumber cut and ready and it will be brought to the local yards of the company on the return trip of the train within the next few days.*

Problems plagued Mr. Dickey, however. The residents complained, "Without the necessary turnouts in various narrow places in the road it is dangerous to life and limb to travel when the traction engines are operating."

The Board of Supervisors reminded Dickey that he had promised turnouts when he was given permission to run the engines, and that he must also strengthen several bridges on the roads, which sagged dangerously under the weight of the machines. By June 11, the engines had broken down and were being repaired at the mill. Dickey promised he would repair bridges and build turnouts before the trains went back on the road.

A month later the engines still sat in the mill yard while experts from the Oakland company tried to repair them. The local companies with their mule teams were happily hauling 40,000 feet of lumber a day from Dickey's mill to Pacific Gas and Electric Company for its Colgate power plant on the Yuba River.[6]

In August, one engine at last arrived in Oroville

pulling four cars loaded with 30,000 feet of lumber, but it was a small and short-lived success. The
enormous costs had far outweighed the income, and
on August 27, the mill closed.

Apparently neither the summer tourists nor the
residents were bothered by the noise of industry and
machinery—nothing is mentioned in diaries or
newspaper accounts to suggest that anyone complained. In fact, business increased.

Falck built several more houses at Woodleaf for
summer guests, and after the toll road company dissolved, he built a large, two-story addition on the
front of the tollhouse for his family. Until that time,
they had lived in private quarters in remodeled
rooms on the southwest end of the second floor of
the hotel. The house still stands across the road from
the hotel, restored to its original appearance and
color in the 1970s.[7]

About 1911, Sophia Falck, then seventy-two years
old, introduced a new contraption to Woodleaf.

Top: *The new Falck home, painted ochre with maroon trim.
The trim was re-painted with a coat of white shortly after
completion. Agnes Falck and her children, Berenice, Helen
and Lawrence, play in the snow in the front yard.*
Bottom: *Portrait of Berenice, Helen and Lawrence Falck.*

Top: *Woodleaf Hotel, 1905. Left to right: Deputy "Zack"; Dan Boland, stage driver; Will Coupe, hosteler; Charles Falck, proprietor; Helen Falck, daughter; Macmanus; Dan Sevey; Mrs. Agnes Falck; Berenice Falck, daughter; George Coppack. "That's me in the torn dress, holding my father's hand. I was into every wagon that came through— there was always something exciting coming into Woodleaf."*
—Helen Falck Dunning
Right: *Advertising card for Woodleaf Hotel.*

FISHING   HUNTING
            CABINS   :-:   CAMPING

WOODLEAF HOTEL
"In Natures Heart"
42 Miles from Marysville on La Porte Road
28 Miles from Oroville
Elevation 3132 Feet

FAMILY STYLE MEALS   WOODLEAF, CALIF.

My grandmother was a remarkable woman—very forward-thinking. She had a water closet installed in the hotel, the first one in the area; it was in the first room on the left upstairs. People came from all around by horseback, buggy or climbing off the stage to see it. They'd all troop upstairs to gather around while someone pulled the chain, the water whooshing in and out. They'd just shake their heads and say they'd never have such a thing in their house.
—Helen Falck Dunning

The entire room was outfitted with new plumbing fixtures. Besides the water closet, there was a huge bathtub with fancy feet, and a wash basin. The room stands out in Helen Falck's memory because it was directly under the crawl space of the third floor, where she and her brother played hide-and-seek with friends. Once, they missed their footing, falling between the rafters through the plaster and lathe ceiling amid a great cloud of dust, noise and debris, landing directly on top of Judge Steele, who was taking a leisurely bath in the tub. She said the noise and racket that followed were much louder, especially from the Judge.[8]

Later the children found a better place to play hide-and-seek—the Coffin House.

It was the best place—dark, with all kinds of places to hide. Downstairs were all the coffins, and upstairs they stored all the trimmings on shelves and in big crates and barrels.
—Helen Falck Dunning

A high point in the day was the coming of the stages, which brought news, mail and travelers. People gathered at the store waiting for the stage to come in, exchanging news, swapping stories and trading goods.

Woodleaf was a hang-out for a lot of characters, and if anything was going to happen, it usually happened at Woodleaf. As far as gold was concerned, there weren't many rich strikes around there, but you could never say for sure. The only way word got out was if somebody started spending like crazy over the bar.
—Jack Dunning

DANCE AT WOODLEAF
Arrangements are being made for the holding of a grand ball on Thanksgiving eve, November 24th. A supper will be served in connection with the affair. Many visitors, including a number of people from Marysville, are expected to attend.

STAGE LEAVES EARLIER
The Marysville-La Porte stage line has started on its winter schedule of leaving Marysville at 3 o'clock in the morning instead of 4 o'clock, which is the time of departure in the summer. On account of the bad roads of winter it takes several hours longer each day to make the trip. The line is operated by J. E. Pauley.
—Marysville Appeal Democrat,
November 19, 1915

The stages had provided regular service for travelers for sixty-five years, but in 1915 one visitor claimed there was no public transportation at all. Special Agent for the Commission of Indian Affairs, John Terrell, was working with the Maidu, who were asking for a grant of land in Strawberry Valley. Since the 1840s, there had been major changes in the policies of the United States regarding the Indians. A vast system of programs was developed, including health care, education, housing, job training and funds for many other projects. Alex Picayune, a Maidu who married Nellie's daughter, Elizabeth, was the leader of the group living in Strawberry Valley and Woodleaf.[9] Terrell's job was to inspect the property that was being proposed for the land grant, but he explains in his letter to the Commissioner in Washington, D.C.:

On reaching Woodleaf, my nearest point to Strawberry Valley, had done considerable walking over a very rough country, no public conveyance of any character to be had going to the Valley, having met all the Indians except an old woman at Woodleaf . . . and have not seen this place offered by Mr. Keith.

Terrell gave his conditional recommendation for

The Falck children playing with friends on the water trough.

the purchase of the property, which was offered for sale for $200. The Commissioner insisted that he look at the property, so in January of the following year he managed to get there, perhaps by the stage-coach or sleigh, complaining,

On the occasion of this visit the entire earth in that vicinity was covered with snow from 18 inches to 2 feet.
(January 16, 1916)

Though reluctant to travel to Strawberry Valley,

Terrell was impressed with the property. He was a persistent advocate for Picayune's group, writing again and again, forwarding letters written by Picayune, and urging the Commissioner to approve the purchase of this property for the Maidu.

They have lived all their lives in the locality . . . acquainted with all the people yet remaining in that vicinity . . . who, when they have work to give, prefer to employ them . . . I unhesitatingly recommend its purchase for them.
(January 18, 1916)

Nellie Johnson (Tasu'mili) draped in bobcat furs, a gift from Al Travis, left.

In 1918 the final documents were drawn up, and the land was placed in Tribal Trust, where it remained until 1958.

The size of the parcel was upsetting to the non-Indians. Though it had a two-story house surrounded by a neat picket fence, a good well, tool-shed, shop and small barn, it was still only a half-acre lot. With all the millions of acres owned by the government, they reasoned, why such a small grant?

The Maidu, however, had chosen the property. Alex had rented the house for nearly a year. The piece of land suited his family, and the owner, who owed five years' back taxes, was willing to sell it.[10] It became known locally as the Picayune Reservation, an ironic name for the smallest parcel of Indian land in the country.[11]

Nellie, together with John and Sarah Kennedy and their children, moved to the Indian land in Strawberry Valley—the last of the Maidu to leave the village of Pakan'yani at Woodleaf. Nellie was well known throughout the towns of La Porte,

Gibsonville, Clipper Mills, Feather Falls, Challenge and Woodleaf. These small communities formed a close-knit group, and she was not only respected among her own tribe, but looked upon by all the people as a wise elder. She knew remedies for poison oak, and the best treatments for burns, fevers and rattlesnake bites. Mushroom gatherers brought full baskets to her home, where she painstakingly examined each mushroom to make sure there were no poisonous varieties. Her baskets were collected by several local families, and in later years she made a complete set for the Mary Aaron Museum in Marysville.

When her husband died, she followed the ancient tradition of her people, and began weaving a basket for the burning. She worked on it for an entire year; when finished, the basket was more than three feet tall. At the burning ceremony she cast it upon the fire to honor her husband. Now his spirit was free to leave the earth and join the Creator, and Tasu'mili was free to continue her life.[12]

Nellie Frances Williams, granddaughter of Tasu'mili.

The "Hoot Owl Picnic" was sponsored by a radio station to celebrate its opening in the 1920s. The station broadcast its program from Woodleaf and provided food and drinks for an all-day party. In the evening, guests danced to the music from the latest records played over the radio. Photograph by Sackrider.

Chapter Thirteen
THE RESORT
1920-1940

Woodleaf Lodge, July 29, 1924
Dear Kid; We came up here two weeks ago and are sure
having a good time. Can't you come up next Saturday?
Edwin is here.
—BERTA

Tourists flocked to the hills during the 1920s. The automobile made travel easier and faster, and every town, no matter how small, put in a gas pump, stocked tire patches and tubes, and learned to improvise to keep the machines running. At Woodleaf, the Falcks installed a modern, glass-topped, hand-operated gas pump next to the store, serving up Associated Gas. Throughout the United States, "rambling" in your own auto became the fashionable thing to do. Oil companies responded with free road maps; states and counties rushed to improve their roads. Resorts, lodges, cottages and cabins were built in the woods of Maine, at the Adirondacks, in the Colorado Rockies, at the beach, and among the redwoods.

Woodleaf, however, was tourist country only in the summer. During heavy rain and snow, the La Porte Road became a muddy morass and was closed to autos. The Marysville-La Porte stage was replaced by a five-passenger Chalmers automobile in 1914, but the horse-drawn stage, sleigh or skis were used in the winters until the mid thirties.[1] Sixteen-year-old Eveline Bustillos set a record in 1913 when she carried the mail twenty-five miles between Strawberry Valley and La Porte, traveling a mile a minute on part of the trail.

As a result of the high rainfall and deep snow, summers were delightful among the lush ferns, wild azaleas and tall trees. Days were warm, rarely hot, and the evenings were cool and invigorating. The emphasis at the Woodleaf resort was on health, sports and relaxation, partly because the Prohibition Amendment in 1919 had outlawed the sale of liquor. Riding horses took the guests along trails to quiet places for recreation and fishing. In 1923, a thirty-by-fifty-foot swimming pool was built in the meadow with a large, sunny veranda alongside; tennis courts were nearby. Falck changed the name of the hotel to the Woodleaf Lodge, replaced the old boardwalk in front with concrete, and bought new furniture for the Lodge and the summer houses.

In 1923, Agnes Falck offered to lease a portion of Woodleaf to the city of Marysville for a summer camp at one dollar a year. She commented that a golf course and lake could easily be added to the facilities, and invited the Marysville people to a picnic at Woodleaf to see the grounds. The road to Woodleaf was unpaved, but a good crowd came to the picnic. The city fathers declined Agnes Falck's offer for a city camp, however. Perhaps the road was too rough. Agnes was quoted by the *Marysville Democrat*:

> *"What's the matter with Yuba County, anyway," exclaimed Mrs. C. L. Falck of Woodleaf yesterday on a visit to this city. "Oroville is getting all the business from up our way," she declared. "That new Butte County highway by way of Bangor is an invitation to our people and those on above to go to Oroville to do their trading, instead of going to Marysville. It's time Yuba County was waking up," she concluded.*
> —April 26, 1923[2]

Despite the condition of the road, Agnes and Charles continued their improvements to the property, and moved some of the buildings to new locations. They closed down the Coffin House, put

WOODLEAF LODGE

VACATIONIST'S AND SPORTSMAN'S PARADISE

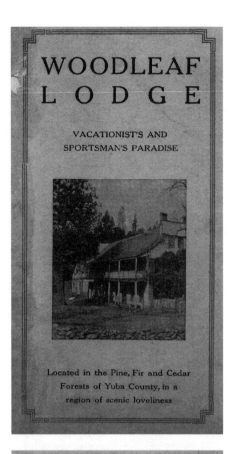

Located in the Pine, Fir and Cedar Forests of Yuba County, in a region of scenic loveliness

Located in the Big Timber of Yuba County, Woodleaf offers every opportunity for recreational diversions and all delights for vacationists and sportsman to be found in a virgin forest.

Woodleaf is very easy of access from the valleys of California, being but 90 miles from Sacramento via Marysville and Bangor. Motorists may also come by way of Oroville and follow a scenic road for 29 miles to Woodleaf. A stage line operates from Oroville to Woodleaf, daily except Sunday. Round trip fare from Sacramento, via Oroville, 30-day limit, $9.95. Round trip fare from San Francisco, via Oroville, 90-day limit, $13.15.

Woodleaf Lodge is on the historic La Porte-Quincy road. This road penetrates a region of great scenic beauty and is the best route from either Marysville or Oroville to Qunicy and Reno, or to the Lakes Basin country near Blairsden.

Persons afflicted with heart trouble will experience no discomfort at the 3,000-foot elevation of Woodleaf.

Woodleaf is a comfortable resort where you can feel at home. An excellent table is a feature and we take pride in our meals. A modern, cool dining room adds greatly to the comfort of our guests. Here you will enjoy a comfortable night's rest in good beds. We have our own spring water, garden truck, berries and milk.

RATES: $2.50 per day; $15.00 per week, single; $28.00 per week, double. Children under twelve, half rate.

Make Your Vacation Count

Come and enjoy a period of rest and recreation in a section where river, lake, mountain and forest have provided a vacantionist's paradise.

For further information and reservation, address

Woodleaf Lodge

Mr. and Mrs. Chas. L. Falck, Props.

WOODLEAF, CAL.

If you would recreate in a forested section where you can fish, hunt, swim, tramp scenic trails and enjoy outdoor diversions, or just rest—come to Woodleaf. Here you will find a section of varied landscapes where you can fish in river, creek or mountain lake; hunt for big or small game in season, or explore a romantic region and enjoy a real vacation. Adjacent to Woodleaf is the Feather River, Yuba River and Lost Creek Lake, all famous fishing grounds. Interesting side trips can be made to Bullards Bar and other historic points, which were famous mining centers in the "Days of Old, the Days of Gold, the Days of '49." Of easy access is the Forest Ranger Lookout Station, which is the only Forest Lookout location in California's seventeen National Forests, which can be reached by automobile. From this point a panorama of scenic grandeur spreads out before you that is worth a long journey.

Woodleaf Lodge brochure of the 1920s.

it on rollers and moved it behind the ballroom, to be used as a warehouse for furniture and supplies. Next, they moved the ballroom across the road where the Coffin House once stood. In place of the ballroom, they built an apartment complex called Sunshine Court. When they were finished, Woodleaf had a new look, and the apartments were full.

The *Oroville Mercury* records the numerous visitors to Woodleaf:

C. F. Parker and wife, Mrs. H. T. Murry and Mrs. C. R. Murry of San Francisco registered at the Lodge Thursday.

Gathered in the famous old bar room of the Lodge Thursday were the fight fans of this section to hear the Dempsey Tunney fight over a radio.[3]

Mrs. Joe Vance and children are now living in Sunshine Court for the winter months.

Mr. Johnson and Mr. Shumway are among the new Standard Oil men now stationed at Woodleaf.
—September 25, 1926

John Hale of Marysville, O. W. Gilmore and E. Eppialy of Hollywood are some of the new arrivals at the Lodge.

The cattle men are rapidly getting their cattle out of the mountains. The cattle are not in as good condition this year as some years. The cattle men say that the young pines and brush are taking all the feed and if the mountains are not burned off it will be useless to take the cattle to the mountains in a few years.

R. L. Whitman of Marysville and R. L. Dillon of Sacramento spent the week end here.
—October 14, 1926

School opened for the summer months Monday with Miss Erma Osgood as temporary teacher.[4] The storms of this week gave us about one foot of snow.

A. A. Littleton, wife and twin daughters, Jean and Barbara of Yuba City and A. A. McMullin of St. Petersburg, Florida spent the past week at the Lodge.

Guests relax in front of Woodleaf Lodge, where a log rail fence surrounds a shady lawn with comfortable chairs and tables. Horses are tied up along the fence, ready for a trail ride.

Top: *The Marysville-La Porte stage and mail carrier Terry Reilly of La Porte.*
Left: *Postcard mailed by "Berta" while she vacationed at Woodleaf. She writes, "Dear Kid; we came up here two weeks ago and are sure having a good time. We take in the dances every Saturday night . . . can't you come up next Saturday? Edwin is here."*

W. Feichter of Los Angeles and Charles F. Foglequist of Berkeley spent several days at the Lodge this week.

The following were some of the guests on Sunday: Mr. and Mrs. H. A. Walton, Frances Switzer, Margaret Berry, Gertrude Cornell and Doris Redbead of Yuba City and Raymond Flanney, E. Forbes, John Ahern, Joseph Brass, Jr., J. Kelley, Mr. and Mrs. George Haney, G. Curran, Mildred and Margaret Yore, Eleanor

Skinner, Margaret Matthews, Frances Sage and Dorothy Hord of Marysville.

Tom Graham of Sacramento who has been at the Lodge for the past week was called back to Sacramento on business.
—March 12, 1927

Nearby towns were caught up in the booming tourist trade. William H. Joy, owner of the Challenge Hotel, sold it in 1924 and built summer cottages in Challenge Park on his new road, Joy Circle. In 1926, he added twenty-five new cottages, and in 1928, a swimming pool. Challenge had a two-story hall, a school, two hotels, the phone exchange, Owls Lodge, stores and shops. The "Days of '49" celebrations attracted two thousand people in 1927, and three thousand in 1928.

Another resort opened near Challenge the same year. Crane Park offered 833 acres with cabins, two streams, a swimming pool, and a golf course. A large portion of the land was subdivided into lots and sold to people who built their own cottages.

Walter Feichter and Charles Foglequist had been coming to Woodleaf for vacations, and saw great possibilities for developing the town. Agnes and

Charles sold the property to them in 1927, but their home and one summer house were deeded back to them as a condition of the sale.

Feichter and Foglequist eliminated any chance of competition with the Falcks by including a clause in the deed that they were never to engage in any business at Woodleaf whatsoever. Falck kept his word and gave up his position with the post office. On August 1, 1927, Walter Feichter was appointed postmaster at Woodleaf.

The new owners built new cottages and new tennis courts; the Lodge was refurbished, and the front area was fenced and landscaped. Surveyors laid out lots for a subdivision, and contractors built roads. In May, 1929, the Woodleaf Lodge Subdivision was

Agnes Falck, Miss Grubbs and Mr. Sewell, the traveling salesman for the Schilling Company, in front of the hotel.

Woodleaf Lodge Sold to S. F. Men By C. L. Falck

recorded, comprising seventy-three lots, two roads and a toboggan slide. The business was so promising that on October 1, 1929, Feichter resigned as postmaster to work full-time at the Lodge and subdivision.

As part of the bargain, Feichter and Foglequist deeded five lots to the Falcks. These were in a choice location along the Oroville-Woodleaf Road.

A few weeks later the New York stock market crashed, and the country's economy, weak from excessive credit spending, overproduction and widespread drought, collapsed. The United States plunged into the deepest depression in its history.

Rich and powerful corporations failed. Families in every social level were forced to give up their homes and farms, repossessed at the rate of 150 a week. There were few social programs, and unemployment benefits soon ran out. In some industrial

areas, half of the people had no jobs, and across the nation unemployment averaged twenty percent—tens of thousands lived on the streets or in cardboard huts. People who had dined at the Ritz only weeks earlier stood in line for a bowl of soup, and tried to sell apples on the street for five cents apiece. Many people tell of living for days and weeks on bread scraps or catsup soup—a spoonful of catsup in a cup of hot water. At one point during the darkest days, someone died of starvation every seven hours. There was no money for bread or flour, much less for leisure and recreation. Across the nation, resorts were abandoned and lodges closed.

As Americans staggered under the hardships of the Depression, Feichter and Foglequist tried desperately to keep the business afloat, but not a single lot in the subdivision was sold. They arranged for Woodleaf Lodge to be used as a health resort operated by a doctor from Oakland. Within weeks, the Lodge was filled to capacity with paying guests, and Woodleaf was alive with music, dancing and midnight parties. The doctor had apparently found people who had money to spend, and it seemed they were making remarkable recoveries from serious illnesses. During one of the Lodge's big parties, the Falcks heard shouts and screams, and looked out to see federal agents surrounding the hotel; people were climbing out the windows and running in every direction. Unfortunately, the doctor was using large quantities of cocaine, bootleg whiskey and gambling as part of his "treatment." From their front porch, the Falcks watched as the guests in their beaded gowns and tuxedos were chased down, arrested, packed into paddy wagons and hauled away. The doctor hid in the kitchen cellar, according to the Falcks, and the agents found him cowering behind the hams and bacon. The Woodleaf Lodge was shut down. Local newspapers were strangely quiet about the raid—some of those arrested were well-known citizens of the valley towns who suddenly "took a vacation," or "were called away on business." Everyone knew who they were anyway, and only a few managed to regain their respectability in later years.[5]

Woodleaf Lodge Subdivision was insolvent. Agnes and Charles Falck took over the property, debts and all. Woodleaf was again in one piece, though heavily mortgaged.

Late one night, flames lit the sky and the old ballroom burned to the ground, then spread to the stage barn, consuming them both. Then fire struck again. The Counts family were camped in Woodleaf while the father worked at the mine. Their stove exploded just as the mother and one child stepped outside the camp trailer. It burst into fire, killing their one-year-old boy and two-month-old twin daughters who were still inside. The Falcks brought the Counts and their one surviving child to one of the summer houses, stocked it with food and fitted them with clothes, and the townspeople helped with the burial of their children.

Falck's daughter, Helen, and her husband, Jack Dunning, moved to Woodleaf to manage the town and help pay off the debts. Helen took the job of Woodleaf postmaster in 1933, and the Dunnings stayed for about six years. When the property was secure, they moved back to their home in Marysville, and Agnes and Charles resumed the management of the town.[6]

Late in 1939, Yuba County surfaced the gravel road between Challenge and Woodleaf. Some of the curves were eased, and the highway was finished in 1940. There were few travelers on this fine new road, however. The stage pulled in with mail, but the tourist business never recovered. It was quiet, indeed, at Woodleaf.

The meadow at Woodleaf across from the hotel; the La Porte Road leading toward Challenge, center; Forbestown Road on the right; a coupe parked by the fountain; the freight barn beyond it; far right, the gate to the lawn area in front of the hotel. (Composite of two photographs)

The Woodleaf mill, 1944.

Chapter Fourteen
THE BIG MILL
1941-1965

The mill building under construction is three stories high and will turn out 100,000 feet of lumber in each shift, employing about 200 men.
—MARYSVILLE APPEAL DEMOCRAT, MARCH 1, 1943

WAR HUNG OVER the world in 1941. The Depression was slowly receding when Pearl Harbor was bombed and the United States was drawn into World War II. Enormous military demands created shortages, and rationing was put into effect throughout the country. Ration books were issued for coffee, sugar, shoes, gasoline and tires, among many other things. Factories stopped producing tennis shoes because of the scarcity of rubber. In December of 1942, there were twenty-seven million cars in America, but only four gallons of gas per driver could be purchased each week.

The need for building materials for military expansion brought a surge in logging and lumbering activity, despite the difficulties of obtaining equipment and machinery. In 1939, only one mill was operating in Butte and Yuba counties, but by the mid forties, there were more than forty-five mills and logging companies. They used a great variety of second-hand equipment, since new machinery was not available.

When the Falcks were approached by Sacramento Box and Lumber Company with an offer to lease the Woodleaf property and build a large mill, they had mixed feelings. It would release them from the heavy demands of maintaining the property, and people would welcome the industry and job opportunities. Fifty-five years earlier the Woodville Steam Sawmill had burned to the ground, and the forest had grown over the charred remains. This new, enormous, modern mill would encompass the entire town rather than a distant corner, and Woodleaf would no longer be a sanctuary for travelers and the

Falck family. Nevertheless, on November 4, 1942, the Falcks finally agreed to a ten-year lease of all their property except the subdivision lots, the family home and one summer cottage.

Earlier in the year, the owner of Sacramento Box and Lumber Company, L. J. Carr, acquired cutting rights to the Soper-Wheeler timber in Yuba, Butte and Plumas counties, and closed his mill in Kyburz, California. By November, the mill had been dismantled and moved to Woodleaf.[1]

Pacific Gas and Electric Company had planned to bring electrical power to the mountain towns during the resort era, but at the onset of the Depression the plans were cancelled. With the arrival of industry and the expected growth of population, crews began stringing power lines from the Colgate power plant. By the spring of 1943, the old diesel generators were retired, and the towns turned on their new, quiet electricity for the first time.

Within months of negotiating the lease of Woodleaf, the Falcks made the decision to sell the town outright, keeping their homes and lots.[2]

WOODLEAF BEING MADE MILL TOWN
That pioneer landmark, the Woodleaf Hotel, where famous and notorious personages stopped in the old days, including stage robber, Black Bart, is being converted into a bunkhouse to accommodate employees of the Sacramento Box Company., which is constructing a great lumber mill and factory here. When weather conditions permit, logging will start, and the five million board foot mill pond will be filled with logs.
—Appeal Democrat, March 1, 1943

Left: *Men in safety harnesses prepare to install the last section of the smoke stack, August 7, 1943.*
Above: *One of the massive steam engines, source of power for the mill.*

A large cookhouse was added to the side of Woodleaf Store, where cooks served 150 men at a time. The hotel's main floor housed a pool hall, saloon, and the mill office. Loggers and lumberjacks bunked upstairs, leaving prints of their hob-nail boots in the floor.[3] The laundry house behind the hotel was equipped with a one-thousand-gallon water heater, and the company employed a man full-time to wash linens and clothing for the cookhouse, hotel and the single employees.

The Sunshine Court apartments housed more workers, with a barber shop in one room at the front. The swimming pool and tennis courts, which had fallen into disrepair during the Depression, were filled in, and movable bunkhouses were placed in the old apple orchard.

Tons of rock were quarried from the hill and spread over most of the meadow, where the mill began to take shape. An excavation at one side of the meadow formed a millpond approximately six acres in size.

The company hoped to attract permanent employees, and family housing was a necessity. L. J. Carr traded with the U.S. government, promising lumber for shipyards and other military needs in exchange for nineteen pre-cut houses. These were built along the roads that followed, in some places, the route of the Woodleaf Lodge roads. Four of the larger houses were erected on the west hill for superintendents.[4]

In addition to the new houses, six summer houses on the east side of town, and five or six more scattered throughout Woodleaf and dating back to the late 1800s and early 1900s, were rented to employees.

The monthly rent was a bargain—$20 for the older homes, $25 for the smaller houses, $30 for the two-bedroom houses, and $35 for the superintendents' houses—gas, water and electricity included.

The mill brought a rich blend of cultures to Woodleaf—Japanese, Swedish, African-American, Norwegian, Mexican, German, English, Native American Indian, and many others. The company reserved certain houses for African-American families, an area called "Colored Town." This was puzzling to small children, for none of the houses in Woodleaf had been painted yet, and the houses weren't colored at all, but were of plain wood, and no different from the rest. Everyone went to the same schools, churches, and stores; the children all played together, and the men worked together. By 1956, all the African-American families who worked at Woodleaf had bought or rented homes in other nearby towns.

In spite of the prejudice of the early years, Sacramento Box had a generous home-maintenance policy for all residents. A full-time electrician, a plumber, a maintenance man, and a garbage collector were employed. If someone wished to add rooms to his home, re-paint, finish a basement room or build decks and porches, he simply made out a materials list, gave it to the secretary at the mill office, and the materials were delivered to the site.

As families moved in, the mill construction continued. By the time the roads into the woods were completed, the pond filled, and the three-story mill finished, Sacramento Box had hired around two hundred men, some fifty short of the crew needed. The war created a scarcity of workers, and many employees worked double shifts in the beginning. On May 4, 1944, the men fired the enormous boilers, the steam engines started and the first log was sawn. It was a day to celebrate.

When World War II ended the next year, however, the celebration was unequaled.

I was only seven years old, but I'll never forget that day. We heard the news over the radio that the war was over. Someone at the mill pulled the cord and blew the whistle, then they must have tied it down, because it blew for hours. Everybody was laughing and crying.
—Dottie Duggan Kearns[5]

A few of the men who worked in the mill, 1943.

The men returning home from the battlefields found steady jobs at Woodleaf. Within a few years, the Sacramento Box and Lumber Company's Woodleaf operation became the most productive mill in the country, with an annual capacity of fifty million board feet.

The self-sufficient operation used sawdust and slashings to fire the boilers, producing steam power on a tremendous scale. One of the steam engines came from Fort Bragg and the other had once provided power for the cable cars in San Francisco; these were replaced with new engines after the war. Power failures were frequent during winter, and surrounding towns were often without power for days. Woodleaf, however, was dark only until the electri-cian had made his way to the main switches that connected the town with the mill's generators. Snowfalls of six feet or more made it a little more difficult.

Steinlage, our electrician was envied during our heavy snow storms for his long, long, legs. However, Steinie even went up to his neck in snow trying to keep the camp in electricity. Steinie was out working the dead of night during the storm, which we all appreciate.
—Splinters, February 20, 1952

The mill ran year-round by stockpiling an annu-al thirty-four to thirty-eight million board feet of

The logs were dumped into the pond using cables placed beneath the load. They were sorted by type and separated by strings of floats, called "log booms," until needed. Background: the highline moves a log onto the cold deck, already more than forty feet high. Beyond the cold deck the hotel, store and cookhouse are completely blocked from view.

Top: *Head rig in mill where first cuts are made.*
Right: *Automatic stacker in mill yard.*

logs in the world's largest cold-deck operation.[6]

The managers, P. V. Burke and George Thompson, took a personal interest in everybody from night sweeper to manager and our families. They really cared about us and we were proud of the mill and town. Even though the work was hard, we had some great times together.
—E. F. Muster[7]

The woods crews of fallers, buckers, loaders, riggers and catskinners were engaged in some of the most dangerous work in the lumber business, and accidents were a terrifying part of life. Two-way radios kept the crews in communications with the office by way of a two-hundred-foot antenna tower on the hill above the pond. Union members purchased and maintained an ambulance in a specially-built garage close to the highway, pointed toward the hospital and doctors forty miles away in Marysville.

The union (C.I.O.) supported not only its own members, but recreation for families. They bought baseball equipment and built a backstop and field in

Fishing along the miner's ditch in the 1940s.

the meadow, where teams from local towns competed with the Woodleaf team. The grassy banks of the meadow were perfect grandstands for watching the ball games on summer evenings, while children played catch and hide-and-seek among the pines.

The remainder of the meadow was used to pasture horses owned by Woodleaf families. One enterprising man made a deal with the owner of a fine string of parade horses, and agreed to pasture three or four horses, saddles and tack included, free of charge during the summer when the horses were not being paraded. The children at Woodleaf had horses to ride and curry throughout the summer, and the stockman claimed the horses in the fall, in prime condition after a season in the wild grass of the meadow.

Trout fishing was a favorite pastime for adults and children, and there were few who did not own a rod and reel. One could walk for miles along the miner's ditch in either direction and never fail to catch trout. The bridges were ideal places to sit on a summer day and watch the swift water take a line down between the shady banks. At the far end of the meadow was an old pond, at one time planned as an

emergency water source, where the trout grew sleek and the water was great for swimming.

In the winter of 1950, after weeks of heavy rain, the hill beyond the last house at the north edge of town gave way, and an area approximately ten acres in size slid into the ravine, demolishing the miner's ditch and filling half the lake with mud and debris. Trees four to five feet in diameter and more than two hundred feet long were strewn in the mud, which continued to slide for several days. By anchoring caterpillars by cable to trees beyond the edge of the landslide, workers finally re-formed the road. The new waterway was lined with a wooden flume for reinforcement. For many years the area remained scarred and barren, and little vegetation grew in the yellow clay exposed by the landslide. The lake below was left to grow wild, but years passed before shrubs and trees grew back to cover the devastation.[8]

Children from Woodleaf attended elementary school in Challenge, and twenty to thirty-five students met the bus each day at the front of the Hotel.[9] High school students rose before daylight to meet the bus at 6:30 a.m., and arrived home from the valley after dark in the evening. They spent three hours a day on the bus, traveling the equivalent of two and a half times around the world during four years of high school.

The county in which students lived determined whether they took the bus to Oroville or Marysville.[10] Although Woodleaf had been in Yuba County for many years, the confusion over its identity continued, and students could choose to attend Oroville or Marysville. Actually, neither district wanted the route. On the first day of school for several years, students waited for the bus at 6:30 a.m., but none arrived. After a week or two, parents organized cars to drive the students to school.

The districts would eventually acknowledge their responsibility, though sometimes weeks into the school year. When a bus finally arrived, it was invariably the oldest vehicle in the district, barely able to creep up the hills and prone to frequent breakdowns. Ironically, the students no one wanted often won the choice awards and honors within the district.

The dilemma was finally solved when Yuba-Feather Elementary School joined Marysville School District. Since that time, only Marysville buses have traveled the route, arriving without fail on the first day of school.

The children found adventure in everything, even the simple task of bringing groceries home from the Woodleaf store. The author was one of the children who dropped everything that floated into the water at the bridge behind the hotel. Running alongside it all the way to our bridge, I leaned far over the water to catch everything and put it back in the sack. Watermelon, lettuce and apples floated. Radishes tended to sink half-way. Oranges went to the bottom of the stream which was about eighteen inches deep, and they were hard to retreive. Cello-phane-wrapped bread floated, but usually the water leaked in on the ends. Years later I mentioned it to my mother, and she said, "You know, I always won-dered why the bread was damp when you brought the groceries home."

There were saloons in every town during the mid thirties and early forties, most of them built after the

Top: *Woodleaf store, post office and cookhouse, 1949; log deck in background. Photograph by P. V. Burke.*
Bottom: *Irene Steinlage photographed her daughter on the front porch of their home, playing with the neighbor's dog.*

repeal of Prohibition in 1933. Each town had at least one, some had two, several had three bars, and there were more in between towns, but it was forty miles from Woodleaf to the nearest church. Challenge townsfolk organized a church and Sunday School, and at Woodleaf the sawyer, Martin Engebretsen, and his wife, Ruth, held services in their home, with a Sunday School in a tent next door.

In 1948, the Sacramento Box and Lumber Company provided the materials for building the white, tall-steepled Woodleaf Church, and members furnished the labor. Roy Brown, head engineer for Sacramento Box recalled:

> *The church bell rang out for every meeting, on New Years, weddings, Christmas, and it could be heard all over town . . . on Christmas Eve families went caroling from house to house through the snow, and when we heard them singing, it was really Christmas.*[11]

Christmas was celebrated with an extravagant

The pathway to the church is shoveled out, ready for Sunday morning.

dinner for employees and their families, given before the mill closed for the holiday. E. F. Muster remembers the generosity of P. V. Burke:

> *Because of the log decks, everybody worked year-round, except for the woods crews. Sometimes they didn't have enough time accumulated to qualify for vacation when the snow ended their season. Burke had them work full-time cutting firewood for the town so they'd get the hours and have a paid vacation with their family.*

The new year came in with a tradition that began in colonial America and is still followed in some mountain communities:

> *One of the wildest traditions in Woodleaf was on New Year's Eve, when all the people came out of their homes at midnight with hunting horns, pans, bells, and every last shotgun, rifle and pistol in town was shot in the air. The mill whistle blew, truck and car horns honked, the church bell rang and dogs howled for about five minutes until the air was full of smoke from all the gunpowder, and the racket could be heard all the way to Clipper Mills.*
> —Anonymous resident

In 1949 and 1950, there were a number of changes in the old town. The Woodleaf store, post office and cookhouse caught fire and burned to the ground during one night in 1949.[12] The Sunshine Court apartments were torn down, and the company built the cookhouse in its place, with a large recreation hall upstairs and pool hall, saloon, kitchen and cookhouse on the main floor.

The Coffin House stood until around 1949, when it was torn down. The inner walls had been insulated with hundreds of cork slabs twelve by thirty-six inches and four inches thick. The youngsters pulled them out and lashed them together to make rafts, using them to ride the creek as far as the falls, about four miles away. The trick was to ride through the flumes where the crosspieces were a couple of inches above your head without getting knocked off the raft or knocked out, and then to bail out

Aerial view of the mill, 1949, before the construction of the dry kiln. Bottom, center, the road to Challenge. The large building at upper left between the log deck and the highway is the Woodleaf store and cookhouse. The hotel and Falck home are obscured by trees. The freight barn is visible to the left and below the store.

before going over the falls. Most often the raft went over, and heaps of broken cork were scattered at the bottom.

Another landmark disappeared when the county improved the La Porte Road at Woodleaf around 1950. The fountain and water trough were torn out to widen the roadway. By 1960, most of the houses and cottages built by the Falcks for summer guests were gone—some destroyed by fire, others torn down.

One of the few mill buildings to survive today is

the dry kiln, built in 1950. The train and tracks are gone, but concrete rail beds remain around and through the kiln where trains shuttled the flatbed loads of lumber. Enormous sliding doors made of steel and concrete closed both ends of each bay, which were filled from end to end with towering loads of green lumber. Intense heat was produced by burning the sawdust and trimmings of the sawmill. Clouds of vapor from the drying lumber poured through the steam vents in the roof. Every eight hours approximately one hundred thousand board

Mill company letterhead and union button worn by shop steward.

feet of lumber was kiln-dried and sent to market.[13]

The increase in the number of employees caused a shortage of parking space, and the old freight barn was torn down. The townspeople tried to save it, reasoning that it could be used as an immense covered parking area for the cars. Nevertheless, the company went ahead with its plan. It was so well-built that it took twice the estimated time to bring it down.

Life at Woodleaf can be glimpsed in the pages of *Splinters*, the newspaper of the Sacramento Box and Lumber Company:

A Job Well Done! Thanks to those employees who answered the Forest Service call for fire fighters at 1:00 PM Saturday and returned at 3:30 AM Sunday. Mr. Sam Grubbs has been released from the Marysville hospital. He was injured while fighting the fire on Poverty Hill.
—September 20, 1950

A son, Elwood Eugene, was born January 16 to Mr. and Mrs. Eugene Bradford of Woodleaf.

Skiing, sledding, a big bonfire and wiener roast was enjoyed one evening by the High School group . . . Bill Dennison, Bill Prater, Benny May, Don May, Gordon Duggan Jr., Marilyn Virden, Emily Engebretsen, Marilyn Wilson and Carol Ann Wilson..
—February 20, 1952

Challenge Cub Scouts met in Challenge, led by Cubmaster Rufus Bond, and assistant Cubmaster, Charles Zirion. Those present were: David Stevens, Morris Wade, David Ransom, John Lang of Brownsville; Carl Hecker and Robert Whitely of Clipper Mills; John Marley and Ted Lindbergh of Challenge; and John Masteller and Bennie Steinlage of Woodleaf.

Woodleaf Church of the Pines services will begin with Sunday School at 10:00 a.m., followed by morning worship at 11 o'clock. Evening services will commence at 7:30 o'clock. Children's church is scheduled for Monday at 6:30 p.m., and Bible study and prayer service will be conducted at 7:30 p.m. Wednesday.

Mr. and Mrs. Vincent Parko and daughters of Woodleaf, left today for Seattle, Washington, where they will visit relatives.
—Marysville Appeal Democrat, April 3, 1954

When the owners retired, Woodleaf changed hands several times, but the mill continued operating. In 1958, it was sold to Woodleaf Land and Timber Company, and in 1962, to a Nevada corporation, Feather River Pine Mills. This corporation's sole stockholder was Georgia Pacific, which in 1963 dissolved the Feather River Pine Mills and shut down the mill in April, 1965.

The shock was felt by hundreds of families in Woodleaf and in the surrounding communities. For twenty-one years the stabilizing effect of the mill had been reflected in the area's excellent school, churches and businesses. As families moved away, the houses were boarded up. The mill equipment was dismantled and auctioned off, salvage companies bid on the remains, and finally bulldozers and fire destroyed the rest. The town was put up for sale.

Woodleaf—the very name rings of home. It is strange that . . . you can't walk down the familiar old road . . . it's a kind of haunted feeling . . .

the mill is gone, the people are gone . . . the people that I knew.
—William E. Sundahl[14]

While the Woodleaf postmaster carried on regular mail service for the few people who still lived nearby, bats and swallows nested in the upper stories of the old hotel. Jackrabbits sometimes hid under the stairs to escape the snow. The empty houses grew shabby and stray cats roamed the streets. Who would buy such a place?

Woodleaf summer staff, 1976. Dave Hatfield photograph.

Chapter Fifteen
THE CAMP
1966-1995

I'll never forget Woodleaf...it was the best week of my life.

—JEFF LOGAN, CAMPER, 1977

G ATEWAY TO Northern California's most spectacular scenic areas," said the brochure from the real estate company, describing Woodleaf. "The heavy snows of winter that fall in the higher elevations, only lightly touch here. There have been times of deeper snows but only on rare occasions," it continued, bringing a smile to those who regularly shovel two to four feet of snow from their porches and roofs. "Brawling streams . . . in the solace of the wilderness" sounded ideal for family camping or conferences. Walnut Creek was among the cities and organizations to send a delegation for a tour. One by one the groups arrived, were shown around, and reported back to their committees. It was too remote or not remote enough; buildings were too close together or too far apart; houses were too old or much too modern. Some found that most of the town was perfect, but they were shocked to see the wreckage of the mill—twenty acres pocked with craters, strewn with broken concrete and twisted metal. The real estate brochure said nothing of this. The mill site alone would require more work, time and money than most potential buyers were willing to spend.

The staff of Young Life Campaign had been searching for property on the West Coast for their camp program for several years. The non-profit Christian organization was founded in 1940, and serves young people in high school clubs throughout the United States and in many foreign countries.[1] Camping activities are an integral part of their program, offering natural beauty, adventure, and time for young people to think about their own relationship to Christ and His relevance to their lives.

Young Life properties in Colorado and British Columbia traditionally hosted groups from California, but they operated at capacity with guests from all across the United States.[2] In addition, because of the distance and expense, many in California could not participate.

In 1965, the Western Staff of Young Life had outlined the features they hoped to find in a property:

A few hours' driving distance from the Bay Area, Sacramento and the San Joaquin Valley for weekend camps, but far enough to have summer appeal; isolated, yet easily accessible; pleasant view desirable; a place that will lend itself to a theme—our ideal is an Old West town.

When Bob Mitchell, the Western Regional Director, heard about the Woodleaf property, he immediately went to evaluate it.[3] Seeing beyond the property's obvious faults, he wrote on November 9, 1965, to the Board of Directors:

I have spent a good deal of time walking over the land and trying to visualize what we could do with it. It is the most desirable property we have found for a dream we have had for several years.

In a report to staff he continued:

The property is the entire little town of Woodleaf, including the post office and church . . . it is filled with tradition, situated in some of the most beautiful country in this part of the state.

Jim Rayburn, the founder of Young Life, made a trip from Colorado to see the land and met with neighbors of Woodleaf. He explained Young Life's goals and ideas for the property, and asked the residents how they felt about having such a group in the community. Carl Sundahl, Woodleaf's neighbor to the northeast, commented,

I thought it was very unusual that Mr. Rayburn cared what we thought. Most people would have just bought the property and done whatever they pleased. I think he knew that a town is different, because so many of us have been a part of it. My wife and I spent our honeymoon in 1923 in the Woodleaf Hotel, and we lived there during the mill years when I was the Yard Superintendent. My sons played baseball on the Woodleaf team. We love that old town, and my wife and I only hoped that whoever bought Woodleaf would be kind to her.

Some people, knowing the condition of the property and the enormous costs ahead, thought anyone who bought Woodleaf deserved only sympathy. The prospect was truly daunting, and it involved much more than the mill site. The owner had discontinued most maintenance programs from 1963 to 1965 because of the impending sale. Some of the buildings were well cared for and in good condition when the mill closed, but had deteriorated rapidly during the year they were empty. Water lines froze and burst, septic systems collapsed, electrical wires shorted during winter storms, and roofs leaked. Only a very optimistic group could envision Woodleaf's possibilities.

The California staff was unanimous in its enthusiasm, and pledged time, energy and funds to the project. On March 1, 1966, with donations from individuals, Georgia Pacific and other companies, the Board of Directors closed the sale and signed the deed. Larry Entwistle of Palo Alto took

Work crew with a load of firewood in one of the new trucks. Photograph by Steve Woods.

the position of property development manager, and Jim Shelton of Oakland coordinated staff program planning.

Staff and volunteers from every Young Life club in California converged upon the town. With shovels, axes, wheelbarrows and wrecking bars they cleared the mill site and tore down structures that could not be salvaged. Bonfires burned almost continuously during the first year. Old trucks and station wagons donated to Young Life were gratefully accepted, and were invaluable in the cleanup and early operation of the camp. "The Crummy" had no lights; the faded pink Studebaker truck was missing several gears, its gas pedal was a short rod protruding from the floor, and it started only on a downhill slope, but these vehicles served the purpose. Since they were used only on private property, their mechanical shortcomings could be overlooked, within the bounds of safety.

In spite of all the activity, the hundreds of bats and swallows that had taken up residence in the hotel were reluctant to move out. When the workers found a stack of bird cages in a truckload of donated goods, they used them for the bat relocation project. A low catch meant extra duty on the kitchen cleanup crew. The bats and swallows eventually gave up and moved to the dry kiln area. But mice, too, had moved into every building, and a list of the early job descriptions included "Town Run, Laundry Run, Mouse-Trap Run." The volunteers were a tenacious lot, and the hundreds of traps were finally added to the bonfires.

In 1967, the Peace Corps contracted to use Woodleaf as a training ground for crews bound for India, an arrangement that provided much-needed revenue for the renovations. The trainees made wooden plows by hand, hitched them to mules, and plowed the meadow. They planted crops that would be grown in India, such as rice, maize and melons. The aroma of curry drifted from the kitchens, and people spoke Punjabi in the streets.[4]

Workers continued the improvements, repairing the roofs and the electrical and water systems, and converting the kitchens to bunk rooms. The cookhouse equipment was sold before Young Life bought the property, so a temporary cooking center was

Bill Styles lived at Woodleaf from 1962 to 1979, an expert at building stone walls and growing giant plants such as sunflowers fifteen feet high. Photograph by Steve Woods.

established in one of the homes on the hill.[5] Three times a day, food was prepared and trucked down to the back door of the kitchen in the pink Studebaker, carried through the swinging doors and served to guests in the dining room, who may have wondered why meals were invariably lukewarm. Kettles and dishes were hauled back to the house on the hill, where the staff used the bathtub as a dishwasher. Bob Mitchell, visiting from Colorado, watched this procession and shook his head, commenting, "If you can pull this off, you can do anything." By spring of 1968, commercial equipment was installed in the main kitchen, and hot food was again on the menu.

The renovation of Woodleaf was intended to reflect its Gold Rush beginnings, using designs and colors typical of the 1850s. The cookhouse was

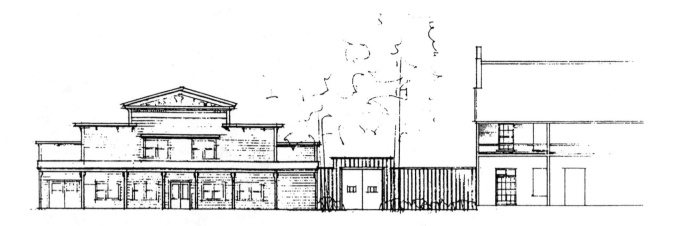

Top: *Plans for the new facade of the dining hall, March 4, 1966. De Witt Whistler Jayne.*
Bottom: *Sailing on the mill pond. Photograph by Kimberly Cooper.*

given an Old West false front and a new name—it was now the dining hall. The saloon and pool hall became an ice cream shop and store called Silver Dollar. Upstairs, the town recreation room was equipped with pool tables, shuffleboards and table tennis. The church was enlarged and a fireplace added, and the building now functioned as the Woodleaf Town Hall for informal gatherings in the evening, while the bell signaled events throughout the day.[6]

The Woodleaf Lodge resort of the 1920s could have inspired the landscaping in front of the hotel. After the asphalt road was removed and rail fences installed, crews brought in truckloads of topsoil, laid carpets of grass and planted flower beds.[7] The trees that remained in the century-old apple orchard were preserved, and the mill pond was excavated, filled with fresh water and stocked with fish. The steady breezes that move up the ravine from Indian Creek make it an ideal place for small sailboats.

Young Life staff planned their camp program for 1968 around Woodleaf's strong points, improvising where shortcomings remained. The game courts and swimming pool were not completed, so the vast concrete foundations of the mill shops were painted with official markings, and basketball standards set up temporarily. Trips to Lost Creek Lake offered water skiing and swimming. The dry kiln was used for corrals and stables, and probably boasted the highest ceilings of any stable in the country. In August, 1968, three week-long camps were scheduled.

I heard the bell ringing on and on, and ran out to see what kind of disaster we had now. The entire work staff—probably thirty-five kids—came running from their jobs everywhere in Woodleaf, changed into clean shirts and lined the length of the fences along the front of town. The buses were coming! When they pulled in, everyone was cheering and singing. They met each person, carried all the luggage and showed them to their cabins. Woodleaf's first real Young Life camp!
—Member of Woodleaf staff, 1968

The activities were fast-paced and challenging, the week full of competition, thought-provoking discussions and outrageous fun. Many young people describe their summer camp experience as "the best week of my life." Those first three Young Life summer camps proved the property would serve its purpose, and set examples of staff creativity and ingenuity that have resolved many later dilemmas.

Late in December, 1968, after weeks of heavy rain, staff families were preparing to take time off for Christmas when the mountain on the north side of town fell away above the site of the 1950 landslide. Don Mossinger (a staff member of Young Life at the time), describes the scene in his journal:

December 21, 1968. The hill behind #10 cabin slid away last night. Took out the side of the mountain, about 6 acres, and filled in the old lake. The ditch is washed out and the ground is still moving. The road to the spring is gone and the camp's water line is completely ripped away. The slide is getting close to the main tank. The whole town is without water. Rained all day.

December 22. Bob Moller [property superintendent] is working with his back-hoe to find the waterline. Cracks opening up in the ground. Backhoe stuck twice—winched it out. Heavy rain through night and most of day.

December 23. Found the water line today, but the ground is still moving, and can't get to it. Heavy rain.

December 24. Light rain. Ground not so soft today. Got to the broken water line and cut it

off. Threaded the end of the pipe and collected all the canvas fire hoses from the whole camp, hooked them up and laid them over the ground with lots of slack. Got the water back to the main line in camp. Flushed out the lines. Water is back to all the cabins, until the hill slides again. Hope it will last through the camp next weekend. Ground is still moving under the hoses. Evening spent with family.

December 25. Took time off today, and we had a wonderful Christmas. All the family came for dinner and stayed the evening.

The makeshift canvas water lines held up for the weekend camp, though the ground still quivered like pudding. When the ground was stable enough, the road to the springs was re-routed, and new pipe lines installed along its upper edge. Luckily, the hill stopped its slide, and the water tank remained in place. The ancient springs still provide Woodleaf's water with a natural pressure system, although, as in the mill days, it is augmented with water purchased from the water district, and recently, with two new wells.[8]

From the time that the old miner's ditch was built, landslides have plagued the company that owns it, causing hundreds of thousands of dollars in damages and loss of water to customers. In 1970, after the second major disaster at Woodleaf, the Oroville-Wyandotte Irrigation District built a siphon across the ravine northwest of the cabins,

The wranglers in front of the old rigging barn, 1976. Photograph by Steve Woods.

*Summer staff girls on the porch of the
Falck House, 1974. Photograph by Steve Woods.*

abandoning the town section. The old miner's waterway, which added so much beauty to Woodleaf, was gone. Eventually the lake, which had become quite small, recovered again as ferns, rushes and willows covered the scars of the landslide.

Woodleaf shared the water supply with the Falck family, and the aging pipelines that ran beneath the hotel and roadways to their homes often failed. Though the Woodleaf staff pitched in with shovels and plumbing work, and helped haul emergency water, upkeep became increasingly difficult. The Falcks sold the small summer cottage, now known as Roadhouse, to Young Life late in 1968, but continued to spend weekends and vacations in the two-story home.[9] In their absence, however, there were frequent break-ins and vandalism, and their holidays were consumed with repair work. With great sadness, the Falcks made the decision to sell their home in 1972, ending nearly one hundred years of ownership, and painfully severing their ties

to Woodleaf. The entire 180 acres were together again, a town in a single parcel of land.[10]

One of Woodleaf's small-town features was lost when the post office was closed in 1971, and Young Life gave up its distinctive address—Post Office Box One, Woodleaf, California. The volume of mail was greater than that of nearby towns, but there were only fifteen permanent box holders and of these, only six actually lived in Woodleaf. Today the mail is directed to Challenge, four miles away.[11]

In some ways, Woodleaf is still a small town, with its own water supply, road and recreation systems and central organization. It is home to the Young Life staff and their families, who are involved in schools, churches and social groups in local communities. Gardens grow in the backyards, children go fishing in the pond and build forts in the woods, and families gather for birthdays and evenings together. But the focus of the townspeople is the daily work necessary to provide the setting for each camp.[12]

Above: *Riding the rapids at Slate Creek. Photograph by Ted Sorensen.*
Below: *Campers arriving at their cabin.*

The town hosts conferences from churches and secular organizations on weekends from September through mid-May, and Young Life uses it exclusively during three months of the summer. Woodleaf manager, Dennis Woll, explains another way the property is utilized:

> *During the spring and fall we lease the camp to Sutter County Schools for their outdoor school program. It runs for nineteen weeks and has proven to be a benefit for everyone involved— the students, their schools, home communities and Woodleaf. They've planted trees on the old mill site and really have enhanced the preservation of wildlife, not only in Woodleaf, but in the surrounding area.*

Woodleaf Outdoor School began in 1969, and now encompasses seventy school districts. Educators in the field of natural science combine studies of

Left: *Rusty, an injured red-tailed hawk, will never fly, but for twenty years she has inspired young people to learn more about all living things. Photograph by John Hendrickson.* Below: *The outdoor school logo.*

ecology with social skills and recreation.[13]

Students can watch wildlife from bird blinds, study the rich aquatic life of the pond, observe plant life under a microscope, learn about the weather and the stars and walk among ancient pines. Birds, animals, insects and plants of many species are found in the study areas, and each one offers a unique environment inhabited by a myriad of interdependent life forms, including human beings. Students discover that there are no easy solutions to the dilemma of balancing the needs of humanity with those of the earth, and the staff encourages the students to examine every facet.

There are field sports, fishing, arts and crafts, hiking and basic wilderness survival lessons during the day. In the evening, students gather for songs, stories, and night visits to Woodleaf's owls.

Throughout the week, the young people meet others from different cultures and lifestyles. The staff reinforce values of honesty, compassion, and respect for others in day-to-day contact, values that will serve the students throughout their lives.

The remarkably vivid teaching that goes on at Woodleaf is one reason why 65% of the local

high school seniors surveyed said their most important educational experience in twelve years of school was Woodleaf. This is learning that lasts.
—Woodleaf Outdoor Education Foundation

The site of a Maidu village was recently discovered by the school director, John Hendrickson, on land adjoining the north side of Woodleaf.[15] The bedrock mortars are situated near a grove of enormous hardwood trees, along with a few conifers seven to eight feet in diameter that survived when the parcel was logged during the 1950s.[16] The grove is considered a fine example of an old-growth hardwood forest. In an effort to save the site, the Woodleaf Outdoor Education Foundation raised funds with the help of the Trust for Public Land, Young Life and thousands of sixth-grade students. The forty acre parcel was secured in a generous arrangement with the owners, the CHY Company. The Woodleaf Preserve will be held in trust for generations to come.[15]

Back at Woodleaf, the students visit the Indian Room, learn Maidu stories and songs, prepare foods with authentic mortars and pestles, and study how the native people lived in their world.

The Outdoor School is recognized nationally as one of America's finest. More than four thousand sixth-graders participate in the Woodleaf program each year, and carry away enduring riches of understanding and appreciation of all living things.

Because Young Life is a non-profit organization,

"You're outside having fun, learning in a different way than if you were just sitting in the classroom with a book," explained a student.

The ropes course challenges summer campers. Photograph by Woodleaf staff.

the fees paid by guests cover only the basic operating costs, and many craftsmen, professionals and students donate their time throughout the year to accomplish a multitude of tasks. In addition, all new buildings and major improvements are funded by donors. This tradition of serving and generosity lies at the heart of Young Life, and of Woodleaf's existence as a camp. In recent years this has made it possible to enlarge the Town Hall and build a new bunkhouse for guests, a dining hall, and a group of Gold Rush-style buildings for the store, ice cream parlor and game room.

Thirty years of Young Life ownership has brought many changes to Woodleaf and more are anticipated:

Woodleaf Town will continue to grow, both in the number of guests—now around twelve thousand each year—and in new buildings. During the next five years a new adult guest lodge, camper cabin and town hall will be added to the property so we can continue to provide the best possible place for kids to come for a week of camp.
—Dennis Woll

In the summer, Woodleaf is devoted to Young Life, whose commitment to teenagers shaped its dream for the town, and whose work saw its fulfillment. In late May, Young Life men and women from across the country join the resident and student staff to prepare the program and welcome the guests, nearly five thousand during the summer. Hundreds of young people arrive for a week of unforgettable adventures. Yet, in quiet places among the great trees and tranquil meadows where the hand of the Creator is clearly evident, there is time to consider another dimension of life—the everlasting treasures of the heart and spirit.

Woodleaf in winter. Photograph by John Hendrickson.

Epilogue

WOODLEAF'S STORY stretches far back in time, the strands weaving a rich and colorful tapestry. The land has sometimes seen mankind at its worst—people driven by jealousy, greed and the lust for power, both in the distant past and in modern times. Travelers from every country have passed through the doors of the hotel, and the old brick walls have witnessed great anguish. There is scarcely a stone in this town that has not been touched by someone's blood, sweat or tears.

But these scenes are mingled with a multitude of others filled with joy and generosity—Maidu men celebrating the first salmon of the season and the women gathering redbud for baskets; fathers working for their families and teaching their children to ski, the names of the trees and the ways of wildlife; mothers taking suppers to families in sickness or death, sewing wedding dresses and giving birthday parties. If we listen to the sounds of the past, we can hear voices of children playing in the meadow; shouts of teamsters and bells on the harnesses of twenty-mule teams straining up the hill; churchbells on a still morning, and through the open windows of the church the sound of people singing hymns; the thunder of a locomotive coming up the canyon and the long wail of the steam whistle; the "dosey-do and circle 'round" sung out to the rhythm of fiddles and banjos as square-dancers whirl in the summer evening.

This ancient land has endured, sheltering and sustaining untold generations. Perhaps the Earthmaker has set aside this small place, a place where we may share the legacy of values that will last beyond our lives—the Woodleaf Legacy.

Maps

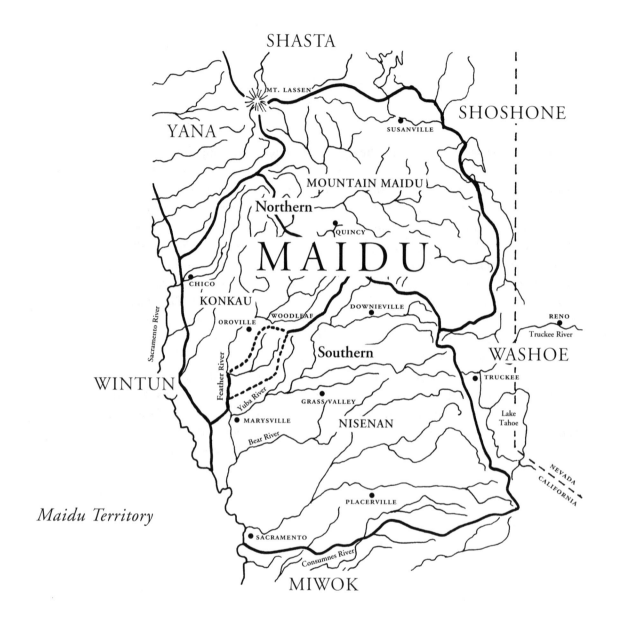

SHASTA

MT. LASSEN

YANA

SHOSHONE

• SUSANVILLE

MOUNTAIN MAIDU

Northern

• QUINCY

MAIDU

CHICO •

KONKAU

WOODLEAF

• DOWNIEVILLE

RENO •

OROVILLE •

Truckee River

Southern

WASHOE

Sacramento River

Feather River

• TRUCKEE

WINTUN

Yuba River

GRASS VALLEY •

Lake
Tahoe

• MARYSVILLE

NISENAN

Bear River

NEVADA

CALIFORNIA

Maidu Territory

PLACERVILLE •

SACRAMENTO •

Consumnes River

MIWOK

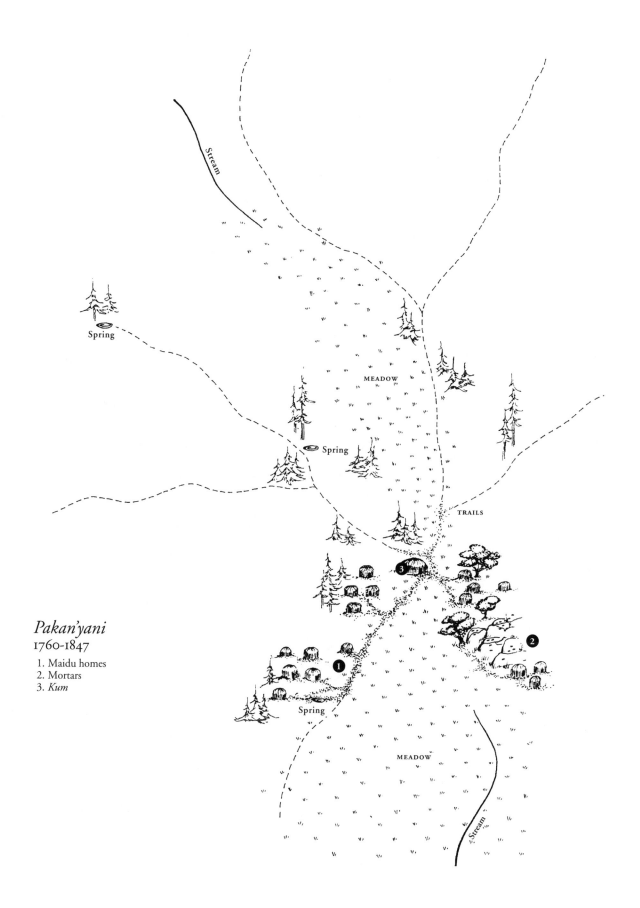

Pakan'yani
1760-1847

1. Maidu homes
2. Mortars
3. *Kum*

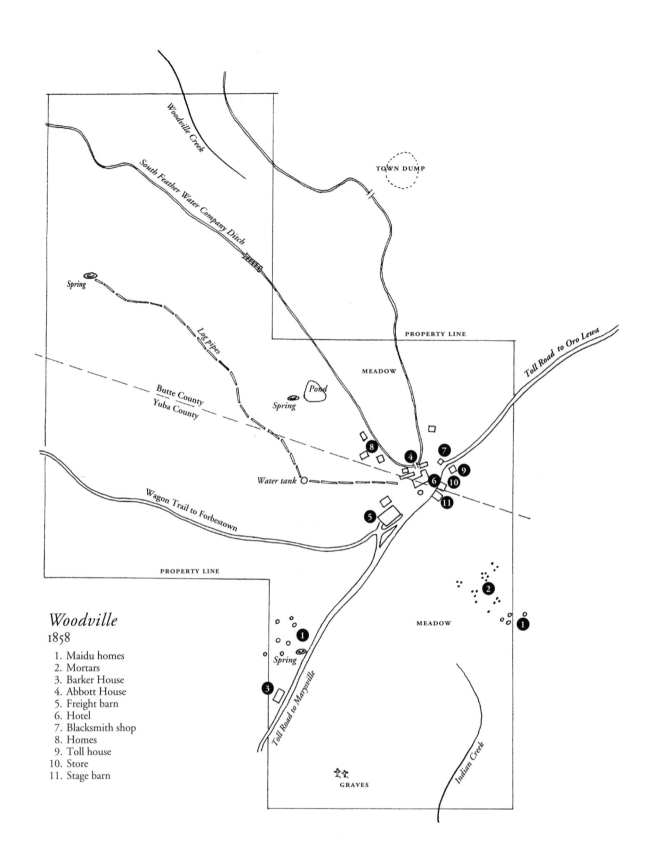

Woodville Creek

Town Dump

South Feather Water Company Ditch

Property Line

Meadow

Toll Road to Oro Lewa

Spring

Log pipes

Butte County
Yuba County

Pond

Spring

Meadow

8

4

7

6

9

10

11

Water tank

Wagon Trail to Forbestown

5

Property Line

Spring

1

2

Meadow

1

3

Toll Road to Marysville

Indian Creek

Graves

Woodville
1858

1. Maidu homes
2. Mortars
3. Barker House
4. Abbott House
5. Freight barn
6. Hotel
7. Blacksmith shop
8. Homes
9. Toll house
10. Store
11. Stage barn

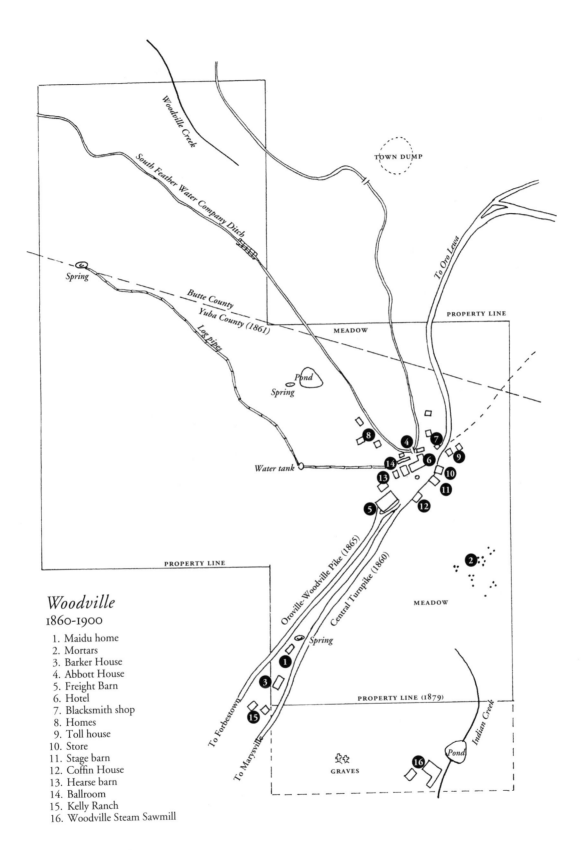

Woodville
1860-1900

1. Maidu home
2. Mortars
3. Barker House
4. Abbott House
5. Freight Barn
6. Hotel
7. Blacksmith shop
8. Homes
9. Toll house
10. Store
11. Stage barn
12. Coffin House
13. Hearse barn
14. Ballroom
15. Kelly Ranch
16. Woodville Steam Sawmill

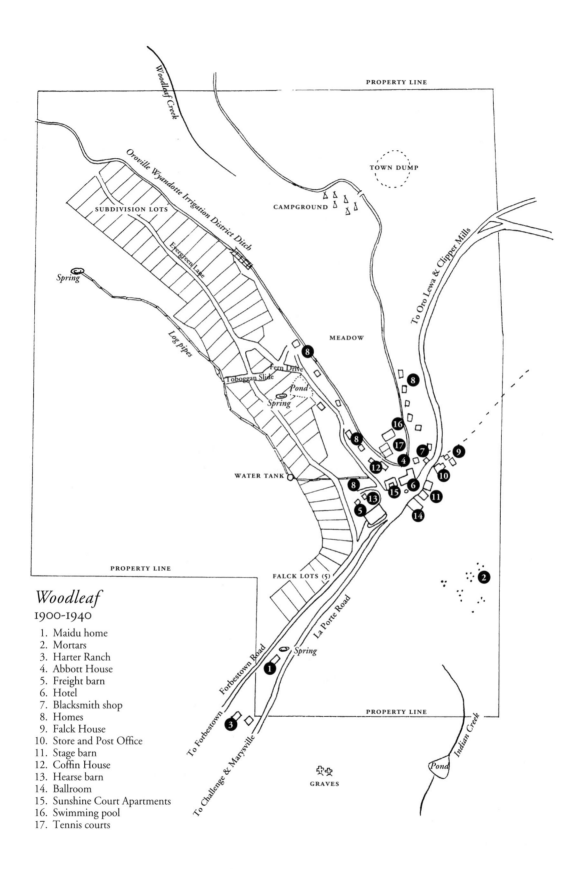

PROPERTY LINE

Woodleaf Creek

TOWN DUMP

Oroville Wyandotte Irrigation District Ditch

SUBDIVISION LOTS

CAMPGROUND

Evergreen Lake

Spring

Log pipes

MEADOW

To Oro Lewa & Clipper Mills

8

Fern Drive

Toboggan Slide

Pond

Spring

8

8

16

17

8

12

4

7

9

WATER TANK

10

6

8

13

15

11

5

14

PROPERTY LINE

FALCK LOTS (5)

2

La Porte Road

Woodleaf
1900-1940

1. Maidu home
2. Mortars
3. Harter Ranch
4. Abbott House
5. Freight barn
6. Hotel
7. Blacksmith shop
8. Homes
9. Falck House
10. Store and Post Office
11. Stage barn
12. Coffin House
13. Hearse barn
14. Ballroom
15. Sunshine Court Apartments
16. Swimming pool
17. Tennis courts

Forbestown Road

Spring

1

To Forbestown

3

To Challenge & Marysville

PROPERTY LINE

Indian Creek

GRAVES

Pond

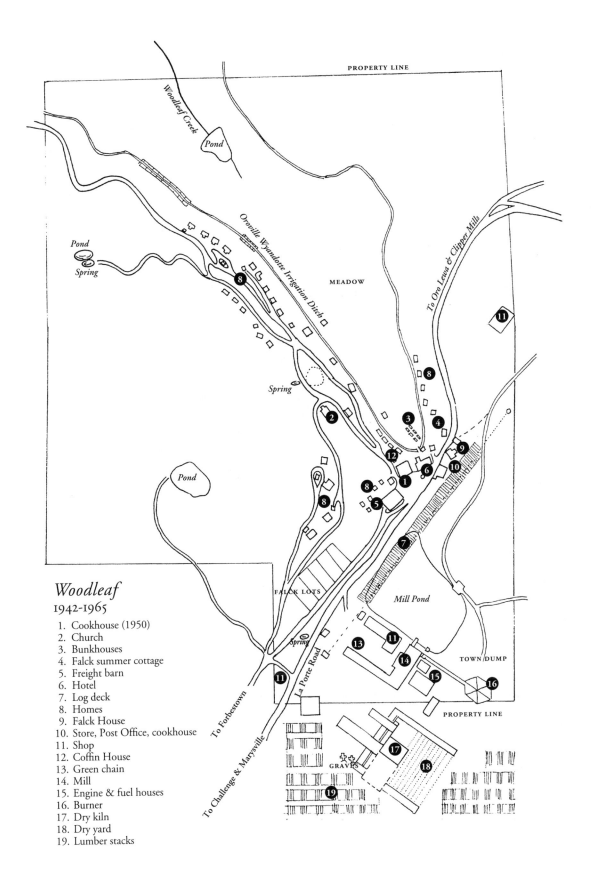

Woodleaf
1942-1965

1. Cookhouse (1950)
2. Church
3. Bunkhouses
4. Falck summer cottage
5. Freight barn
6. Hotel
7. Log deck
8. Homes
9. Falck House
10. Store, Post Office, cookhouse
11. Shop
12. Coffin House
13. Green chain
14. Mill
15. Engine & fuel houses
16. Burner
17. Dry kiln
18. Dry yard
19. Lumber stacks

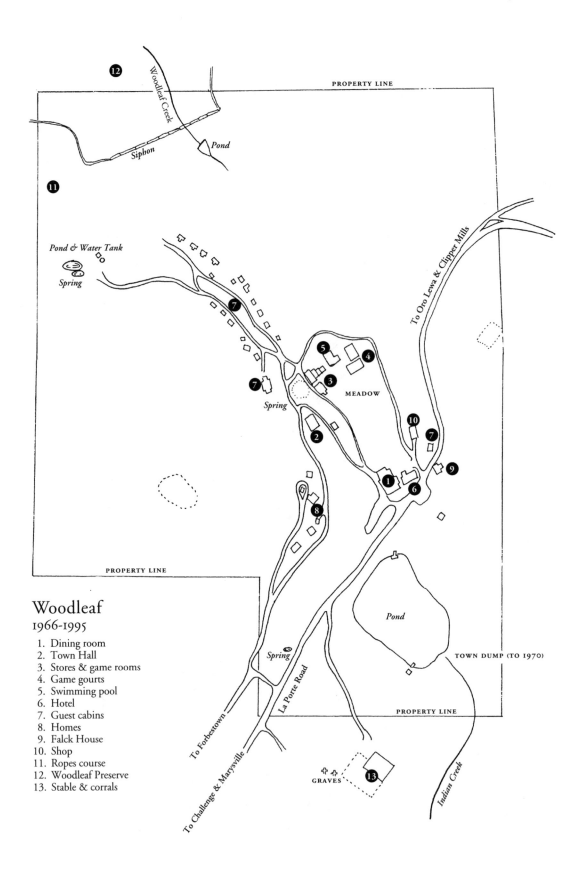

PROPERTY LINE

Woodleaf Creek

Siphon

Pond

Pond & Water Tank

Spring

To Oro Lewa & Clipper Mills

MEADOW

Spring

PROPERTY LINE

TOWN DUMP (TO 1970)

Pond

Spring

La Porte Road

To Forbestown

To Challenge & Marysville

PROPERTY LINE

GRAVES

Indian Creek

Woodleaf
1966-1995

1. Dining room
2. Town Hall
3. Stores & game rooms
4. Game gourts
5. Swimming pool
6. Hotel
7. Guest cabins
8. Homes
9. Falck House
10. Shop
11. Ropes course
12. Woodleaf Preserve
13. Stable & corrals

Notes

CHAPTER ONE

1. Sophia Hedstrom Falck (1839-1912) told her grandchildren that the Indians called this place "Pakan'yani." The linguists R. B. Dixon and William F. Shipley, writing separately, list *pakani* as a form of the Maidu word for "springs" or "marsh," and most sources state that *yani* means mountain

    The Maidu name for Strawberry Valley is Pomingo, said to be the name of a plant that was gathered there (Thompson and West, p. 97). I was unable to find the Maidu names for other local towns or places.

2. Different theories are proposed by anthropologists and linguists concerning the Maidu arrival in this area. William F. Shipley and Richard A. Smith base their theory on linguistic evidence.

3. The Falck family was told by Tasu'mili, a Maidu woman born here in 1827, that before the white man came about 130 Maidu lived in this village. This would place it well within the size believed by Kroeber to be average for Maidu villages, with a range of between 125 to 500 people living in and around the area. Tasu'mili was only a small child of five or six when the epidemic of 1833 occurred, and it is not known whether she could have recalled the size of the village, or whether she had been told of it. Moreover, we do not know whether this was the population before or after the epidemic.

4. The name of the main tribe, Maidu, is used throughout this book for the sake of clarity, although there are three separate divisions (see map, p. 149). According to Kroeber, the ridge between the Feather and Yuba rivers was the approximate northern boundary of the Nisenan territory. To the north were the Konkau Maidu, and to the northeast in the high country, the Mountain Maidu, both groups belonging to the Northern Maidu. Pakan'yani lies directly on the center of the ridge between the Yuba and Feather watersheds. In 1902 Merriam described the territory in detail, naming the Challenge-to-Strawberry Valley areas as belonging to the Northern Maidu. The people of Pakan'yani traveled regularly into the areas to the north, and many of them intermarried with those groups. The languages were mutually intelligible, while the Indians of this area stated they could not understand the Southern Maidu (the Nisenan). (For description of territory, see Merriam, p. 313.)

5. The common currency among the Maidu was the disc bead (clamshell), obtained in trade with the Pomo. It was usually in rough form of broken pieces, drilled and strung. The Maidu then finished the clamshells by grinding the strands in grooves of stone until the pieces were disc-shaped. This increased the value of the money—a good return on their investment. In 1875, a bead one-third of an inch in size had an approximate value of five to the dollar. Large one-inch beads were four to the dollar. Dentalia shell was highly valued, and was too rare in the Maidu territory to be used as money, but was used for jewelry and ornamentation (Kroeber, p. 421).

6. Mariah, a Maidu, was taken by the Yahi tribe when she was fourteen years old, and kept as a slave to the chief's wife. She escaped and hid in caves for days, eventually finding her way back to her people. The story is related by Mariah's granddaughter in Potts, pp. 40-42. Many other tribes engaged in similar slave practices. The Achomawi, Klamath and Modoc of California traded slaves to the Chinook at the intertribal market at The Dalles in Oregon (Kroeber, p. 308). The Shastas and Yuroks had slaves who were prisoners of war or debtors (Kroeber, p. 296). See also Note 3:14.

7. The *kum* was located on the site of the present-day parking lot west of the hotel (see maps, pp. 150, 151).

8. "Wonomi" is translated as Immortal One.

9. Kajnahu was the name of Dan Williams, a Mountain Maidu who lived in Quincy. Not all Maidu names were given by tribal elders or parents. According to William F. Shipley, Kajnahu purchased his name when he was a boy from an old Pomo Indian around Healdsburg in exchange for a bow and a quiver of arrows. Shipley recorded this creation story as Kajnahu told it in the 1950s.

10. According to Hill, the varieties of flora and fauna used by the Maidu for food, shelter, clothing, tools and medicine include 184 flora, 38 mammals, 49 birds, 15 fish and 11 insects. Worms, grubs, larvae and grasshoppers were commonly eaten, but the dog, wolf and coyote were regarded as poisonous, and Kroeber states that buzzards and all reptiles and amphibians were strictly avoided as food.

11. According to Merriam (p. 314), "Maidu kept two kinds of dogs—coyotes and cross-foxes. . . . They were easily trained and tamed." Kroeber disagrees (pp. 215, 216), explaining, "the Indians state that their dogs were of all colors, yellow, red and black . . . [which] argues long domestication and the probability of a disposition very different from that of the wild ancestor," not merely tame coyotes or foxes.

12. Maidu mortars are funnel-shaped, pointed at the bottom, and usually in bedrock. There were people even before the Maidu, but almost nothing is known about them. The Maidu called them Bete'ito, or "first people," and the only traces they left were globular-shaped mortars regarded with veneration and awe by the early Maidu (Dixon, p. 412).

13. Marie Potts (Chankutpan) was born in 1895 in Plumas County, educated in Pennsylvania, and reared five chil-

dren. She played a key role in establishing the American Indian Press Association and was co-founder of the Federated Indians of California Inter-Tribal Council. In 1975 she was honored by the state of California for her efforts to help the Indian people. Her name, Chankutpan, means "one with sharp eyes." Although she was a member of the Mountain Maidu and lived further north, her experiences parallel those of the Maidu who lived in Pakan'yani.

14. According to Kroeber, the Maidu have two names for houses. The *kum* is the larger structure, and could be a dance chamber, a sweathouse and a dwelling. The *hubo*, a conical bark structure, was used only as a temporary dwelling. The uses and names varied among different groups, and some used the word *kum* for all structures. Their dance chamber or house of worship is also called a roundhouse.

CHAPTER TWO

1. The Maidu population before the epidemic is estimated to have been somewhere between 9,000-27,000. A. L. Kroeber, in his examination of the depopulation of the native Americans, places the figure at around nine thousand. (Kroeber, pp. 394, 395.)

2. The secret nature of a personal name is related in Powers, p. 104, but the practice varied from place to place.

Helen Falck Dunning (1906-1991) said her grandmother would not permit anyone to speak the name Tasu'mili when the Maidu were present, deferring to their custom. Helen did not know the Maidu names of Tasu'mili's children or others in the family, but knew them only by their American names.

According to Powers, most names for women were those of animals and birds. It has not been possible to verify the meaning of the name, Tasu'mili, for several reasons. The language of the Maidu is quite complex, and not only are there three major divisions (Nisenan, Mountain Maidu and Konkow), but numerous separate dialects in each division. Powers noted while traveling in this area that a new language had to be dealt with every ten miles. As far as is known, there is no "pure" language left of any one dialect due to the epidemics of and preceding 1832-33 and the dispersal and annihilation during and after the Gold Rush. In addition, there were secret languages used only by the medicine men and women.

Powers points out that many Maidu names, as in other cultures, were made up of syllables chosen for their pleasing sound and may have no specific meaning, except those they might eventually acquire through association. Names could also be bestowed at any age because of some event in the life of the recipient, and a person could have two or three names. As Shipley relates, sometimes a name was acquired in trade or was purchased (Shipley, pp. 131, 132).

When a person died, his name could not be spoken, so the names of ancestors may not be known, except where the taboo is not observed. If a child was given that name it was freed from its association with the dead, and could again be spoken, except, as related above, in that person's presence.

The name of Tasu'mili's father, Ya'lo, was learned from one of her descendants who still lives in the area. It was also listed on a document signed by a descendant in 1928, found in the National Archives in Washington, D.C. Her mother's name is not known. Tasu'mili's date of birth varies in different sources, and I have used the date given by her family and by the Yuba County Archives. Another name is given for Tasu'mili on a document signed by her son, John Kennedy, in 1928—Pupow'doli.

3. Dixon states, "As early as 1820, or possibly even earlier, . . . the trappers of the fur companies had in ten years, explored much, if not all, of the area occupied by the Maidu" (p. 129).

4. Work's expedition was not the first to be sent out after Smith's visit to the fort, but took place several years later. The Hudson's Bay Company is the oldest continuously operated commercial company, founded in 1670 and still in business today.

5. The total includes Work and his father-in-law, Pierre Legace.

6. Michel Laframboise (also spelled Michele La Framboise) eventually became an American citizen, and lived in Oregon. He was known as the "Captain of the California trail," making his last official trip in 1843. He visited California frequently, the last time around 1849-1850.

7. French Camp near Stockton was the site of the annual rendezvous of American trappers, and later a settlement of Hudson's Bay Company people.

8. Some historians believe that malaria was brought into the country by sailors during the period of 1830-33, and point out that there was a great epidemic in Oregon prior to the one in California.

9. In spite of the intense competition, trappers traded goods with each other, with the Russians at their fort (established in 1812), with the Franciscans at the missions, and with the Spanish at their presidios in Monterey and San Francisco. In emergencies, they shared food and other supplies.

10. Work explains that the kill "is certainly a great many more than was required, but when the most of the people have ammunition and see animals they must needs fire upon them let them be wanted or not. The animals for a considerable time back have been in general very lean, indeed they could not be expected to be otherwise being hunted without intermission." The meat was dried to provide food when they could not find game, but still, the quantity is staggering in view of the fact that this was only one of many trapping expeditions in California.

11. There were no trading posts in the mountain regions surrounding Pakan'yani, and the trappers traded

directly with the Maidu during their trapping and hunting treks. Theodor Cordua, a German immigrant, leased land from Sutter and ran a trading post near the present town of Marysville, and recorded his dealings with both the valley Indians and the Hudson's Bay trappers during the early 1840s, but this was well outside of the territory of the Maidu at Pakan'yani.

12. Tasu'mili's story of the trappers' visits and the trade beads was first related to me by Helen Falck Dunning, who heard it from her grandmother, Sophia Falck. Pearl Logan confirmed portions of the story, recalling that her grandmother, Tasu'mili, had spoken of the white men coming and the trading that took place in the village.

13. There is conjecture among some anthropologists and historians as to the specific diseases that caused these catastrophes, but most agree that malaria was the biggest killer in 1833, based on detailed descriptions of the symptoms given in diaries, letters and reports. Other epidemics before and after that time were caused by cholera, smallpox and malaria (Cook, p. 308).

14. John Work (originally spelled "Wark"), enrolled in the Hudson's Bay Company in 1814 when he was twenty-two years old, and rose through the ranks, serving in many positions of leadership, and as a member of the Legislative Council of Vancouver Island. He and Josette and their eleven children (possibly more, since only those surviving past infancy are recorded) eventually settled in Victoria, first in a log home, then in a large mansion. John often strolled about the town, his pockets full of sweets for the children who followed him about. He died in 1861, after suffering a relapse of malaria, or the lingering effects of the disease. Josette lived until 1896, surrounded by children, grandchildren and friends.

15. The Russians, who had occupied the land since 1812, sold their cannons and supplies to Captain Sutter when they disbanded their colony and fort on the north coast.

CHAPTER THREE

1. Jonas Spect wrote of his discovery and included a small map showing where he first found gold (Spect letter, Huntington Library). When he arrived in 1848, of course, the town of Timbuctoo did not yet exist. In the letter, written in 1879, he uses the names that were later given to the locations. He was born in Pennsylvania, and in 1847 left Independence, Missouri for the Oregon Territory, driving an oxcart alone. He came to California before gold was discovered, and left the mining area shortly after finding the nuggets on the Yuba River, eventually becoming a state senator from the Sonoma district. (See Thompson and West, pp. 36, 83.)

2. The value of exports from California in the years before the Gold Rush are calculated at well over one million dollars annually, and consisted of hides, tallow, lard, wheat, soap, timber and furs. They were shipped mainly to England, Russia, France, America, Mexico, Peru and Hawaii.

The vast ranchos in the fertile valley produced grapes, wine, olives, figs, almonds, peaches, oranges, cotton, flax, corn, hemp and tobacco, but the main industry was cattle. The yearly slaughter of 100,000 head was worth $800,000, and ships from many countries came into the bay at Yerba Buena (later San Francisco) to trade.

3. Prices varied widely, changing at a moment's notice, and these are only a few examples. In 1852 immigration reached an even higher peak than 1849, and the prices of essential items such as flour, pork and shovels also peaked during that period. In San Francisco there were eight major fires between 1849 and 1852, destroying warehouses and merchandise stocks. When the customs house and warehouse burned in 1849, the price of American brandy doubled within a month. In the fire of May 1851, twenty-two city blocks burned, with losses of between seven and fifteen million dollars. Prices of building materials, cloth and clothing rose seventy to eighty percent. Bad weather greatly affected the prices as well, and at times goods reached ten to twenty times their cost by the time they were hauled to the remote areas. The cost of hauling the goods was added to the price. In the Yuba area in 1850, miners paid three dollars per pound to men who would pack goods in to their camps on their backs through twelve- to fifteen-foot snows.

4. Isaac E. Brown was a Justice of the Peace for a time in Keystone Township in Yuba County (Keystone later became New York Township), and a California State Assemblyman in 1870 and 1871. He declared himself a "Farmer and Miner" of two hundred acres in Brownsville in an interview in 1879. He is buried in Brownsville Cemetery (Thompson and West, pp. 21, 42, 91, 92, 96, 121, 131, 142).

5. Many of the meadows in and around Brownsville, Challenge, Clipper Mills, Forbestown, Woodleaf and other places throughout the area were the sites of Maidu villages.

6. On a survey map of 1853, the creek south of Barker House is simply labeled "Barker's Ravine." It is believed that Barker named Indian Creek. It is not known who first named Slapjack Creek. Slapjacks were made of flour and water and could be cooked quickly over a campfire using any available animal fat. Downie was describing the camp at Foster's Bar, but no doubt many of the mining camps smelled the same in the early morning.

7. Cut-Eye Foster's Bar and Foster's Bar were miles apart, but both were on the North Fork of the Yuba River.

8. In the first edition of *Woodleaf Legacy*, the information about the location of the Barker House was gathered from Thompson and West's *History of Yuba County*, 1879, the earliest published history of this area.

There are many indications, however, that Barker House was located elsewhere. 1) A map of 1851 shows Barker House southwest of the junction of the trails to Marysville and Oroville. 2) A diary entry written by Twogood while he lived in the Woodville tollhouse reads, "I walked to the old barn, down to the old Barker Place." This was written by a man who thought nothing of walking to Forbestown or Strawberry Valley for church or a lodge meeting, so it is unlikely that he was describing a walk across the street. 3) A letter from J. W. Pratt notes, "In the fall of 1851 a meeting was called at the Barker House, location, a short distance below Woodville, to form a joint stock company." 4) Another diary entry by Twogood, December 3, 1878: "The Kelly house is going up, down near the old Barker House that used to be." An 1853 survey map for a turnpike in the California State Archives, which clearly shows Barker House a few hundred yards southwest of Abbott House, at last provided clear evidence of its location. On this map, Abbott House is approximately where the hotel stands today, at the junction of the two trails leading to the valley. The trail to Forbestown and Oroville followed a different route in 1853, traveling northwesterly over the hill. (See maps, pp. 151, 152.)

9. William J. Organ came to California overland in 1849, and his memoirs have been handed down in his family. Kathe Goria-Hendrickson of Clipper Mills, a staff member of the Woodleaf Outdoor School, is a descendent of Mr. Organ.

10. San Francisco was called California's "First City," Marysville was "Second City," Sacramento, "Third City." Not until a few years later did Sacramento overtake Marysville. The courthouse in Marysville was a two-story canvas house measuring twenty by thirty feet.

11. The men who first settled Rough and Ready had served in the regiment of "Old Rough and Ready" (General Zachary Taylor) during the Mexican-American war.

12. The records of this period, including those of the *alcalde*, the Spanish or Mexican leader (mayor) in Marysville, are preserved in the Yuba County Archives.

13. According to the terms of the Treaty of Guadalupe Hidalgo, the United States honored the land grants made by Spanish and Mexican governors. Those who lost land, including Captain Augustus Sutter, who lost a major portion of his holdings, had acquired grants from former governor Micheltoreno in 1845 after he was expelled by revolution.

14. The enslavement and slaughter of people during war and invasions reaches back to the beginning of recorded history. The ancient Sumerians in 5,000 B.C. enslaved prisoners of war, and in Greece, 90% of the population was once composed of slaves captured in neighboring countries. Spain enslaved many of the Aztec, Inca and Mayan people, who had also built their empires on slave labor. Tribal chiefs and kings on the coasts of Africa supplied foreign traders with slaves by raiding the inland countries and villages, and kept slaves of their own. See Note 1:6 regarding slavery among American Indians. According to historians, the word *slave* came from the Slavic people who were taken in bondage by the Avars, and later in the Middle Ages by the Moors and Franks.

During the twentieth century many countries abolished slavery—England in 1833, France in 1848, Holland and Russia in 1860, United States in 1863, and Brazil in 1888. In spite of the fact that slavery was abolished in the United States in 1863, an estimated 3,000 to 4,000 Indian children were taken as slaves in the period of 1852-1867.

Slavery remains a part of the culture in Mauritania, North Africa and other countries, and the mass killing of tribes, ethnic groups and people of different beliefs continues in the world today.

15. The use of "spruce" bark is mentioned by diarists, but actually refers to Douglas fir bark. There was confusion among early botanists in identifying this tree, since it resembled both fir and spruce, but it is actually a distinct species. John Muir described a wild storm in Brownsville in 1874, when he "rode" a "Douglass spruce" tree. (See also Peterson's *Field Guide to Western Trees*.)

16. There is conflicting information about the founders of the South Feather Water Company. In Thompson and West's *History of Yuba County*, E. Goble is said to have formed the company, and he was also the proprietor in 1879. However, in Mansfield's 1882 *History of Butte County*, the founders are said to be Bartholomew and Gaskill. No records of the company have been found in Butte County Archives, but Bartholomew's diaries and other documents of the early 1850s describe in detail his business dealings and partnership in the water company with Gaskill. The company merged with Forbestown and Union Canal in 1907, and later became part of Oroville-Wyandotte Irrigation District (Bartholomew Diaries, Lilly Library).

17. Bancroft estimates that 42,000 came overland, 23,000 came by sea from the U.S., and 16,000 from Europe in 1849. Ninety thousand people returned to the States via Panama in the period between 1849 and 1851. The total number of people coming overland after that time was much smaller, but the number arriving by sea remained considerable.

CHAPTER FOUR

1. Two sources of the Gold Lake story are Bancroft's *History of California* and Thompson and West's *History of Yuba County*. Stoddard's name is given as Stoddart in some sources. He apparently adopted the title of "Captain" without the benefit of military service.

2. Onion Valley is in Plumas County, above La Porte.

CHAPTER FIVE

1. Jumper's mill is listed in the Yuba County Assessments

for 1852 as "Berry, Jumper and Company Mills." Jumper soon sold out to Peppus, who remained in the lumbering business for many years. The spelling of Peppus varies in documents, and is sometimes spelled Pepper.

2. Research has not revealed the fate of Amos A. Hill. George Hill appears in various records, such as the Yuba County Assessments (1852), and the Miner's Poll Tax (Yuba County Archives).

3. The *Sacramento Union* article is quoted because there are no copies of the February, 1852, *Marysville Herald* in the California and U.S. Library systems, National Archives or Library of Congress. In fact, all the issues from July, 1851, to August, 1853, are missing. We know the article was drawn from the Marysville paper, as it is prefaced with the title, "Up-River News," and the sentence, "We are indebted to Gregory for a copy of the *Marysville Herald* of yesterday."

   Mt. Hope was a settlement west of Barker House, on the trail later developed as the Oroville-Woodville Pike, at the Thurston-Grubbs' property.

4. The Falcks (Agnes, Charles and Helen) knew that the two men buried at Barker House were "a preacher and a miner," although their names had been forgotten. When I found the newspaper article describing the tragedy, I thought at first that Kerns might be the miner buried at Barker House, but the name tugged at my memory. Then I recalled that when I was a child I saw a hand-cut stone on the grave of a man named Kerns who was killed by Indians. The gravesite is at least seven miles from Woodleaf. I went back to the spot and photographed the stone, but still had no clues as to the identity of the others. With the discovery of the Pratt letter, it was clear that the men killed near Woodville were William Sherman and D. B. Day, and that they are "the preacher and miner" buried here. The graves were buried under gravel and rock fill from the quarry, brought in by Sacramento Box and Lumber Company in 1942. There is a third, unmarked grave at Woodleaf, but nothing is known about who was buried there or when. It may have been the grave of one of the "unknowns" mentioned in Pratt's letter. The hanging tree was on the south side of the road, but it was gone long before the turn of the century.

5. Concerning the Maidu tradition of revenge for a death, Powers states that revenge had to be taken within twelve moons after the murder (Powers, *Tribes*, p. 106).

6. Tasu'mili stated that the chief of her tribe in 1852 was named Yon'ni (National Archives), but there is no record of the names of the Indians who were killed. There are many tragic stories handed down about the Maidu and the whites; this is the only one concerning Barker House that could be verified.

7. L. T. Parlin signed as a witness when Amos and George mortgaged Barker House, on April 24, 1852. The original document is part of the dossier of *Farr v. Hill,* Yuba County District Court, Yuba County Archives. Sarah Parlin's gravestone reads, "Thy smile once filled a home with gladness."

8. Millions of tons of sediment settled into the Bay, wiping out the oyster industry in the first major environmental disaster for this sixty-mile long estuary. During the 1860s, eastern oysters were introduced to try to re-establish the oyster industry, but unfortunately along with them came a pest called the oyster drill, as well as other alien species, circumventing the plan.

9. By the spring of 1853, California's population was 300,000, and $260,000,000 in gold had been taken out of the hills. This figure is calculated at the rate of $16 an ounce, the price of gold in 1853.

10. For a number of years all documents pertaining to Barker House/Woodville were recorded in both Butte and Yuba counties. The discovery of additional documents now dates the ownership by Joseph and Susan Wood from 1853 instead of 1856, as previously believed.

CHAPTER SIX

1. Records show that the name "Abbott House" was used from 1853 to 1855, then was combined with "Woodville House" for another eight years, but Abbott House was never mentioned in prior histories. In the records, two or three names are used to confirm the identity of the property until 1863. With the sale to James B. Kelly that year, the first two names are dropped, and it is recorded as "Woodville" until 1898.

2. The freight business between Marysville and La Porte reached a peak in 1859. It began to decline gradually thereafter, due to the decreasing yield of gold, though it continued to be an important commercial factor until 1884-1893, when hydraulic mining slowed, then stopped.

3. Wells Fargo was an express company at this time and not a stage company in this area. Later they did buy the Pioneer Stage Line, but as far as is known, did not own stages on the Woodville route. The express companies contracted with stage lines (on this route, McLaughlin's and the California Stage Company) to carry their express boxes, in which letters, packages and gold were sent from town to town. Sometimes the words "Wells Fargo" were painted on the side of the stage together with the stageline name, but this only indicated that the stage company carried Wells Fargo express, not that the stage belonged to Wells Fargo. (Similarly, "U.S. Mail" was sometimes lettered on the side if the stage carried the United States mail.) If the shipment was particularly valuable, an armed Wells Fargo agent or messenger accompanied the express box, riding with the driver.

4. The man who discovered the pass was named Beckwourth or Beckwith. Both the map of California released by the State Surveyor General, Eddy, in 1854, and the U.S. Geographic Board, Sixth Report, 1933,

shows "Beckwith Pass." The name "Beckwith" was used when he was a roustabout on Mississippi River steamboats, or living with his adopted Indian tribe, and working for the American Fur Company. It became "Beckwourth" when his biography was written in 1856.

5. The Wood family home is in Gallia County, Ohio, but the ownership has passed out of the family.

6. Many articles and references in county histories state that the builder of the hotel was James Wood, including one article published in 1991 in a local newspaper. These errors all stem from repeating mistakes in the *History of Yuba County* by Thompson and West. On pages 89 and 96 the builder of the hotel is said to be James Wood, but his name is given correctly on page 143. Joseph Wood is the correct name, taken directly from property deeds, ledgers, county documents, family records and other primary sources.

7. The Woodville post office was in Butte County, but there are no site reports in the National Archives that give its exact location. It may have been in the Butte County end of the hotel or in another building on the Butte side of the county line.

Woodville was by no means granted the first post office in the area—as early as 1851 there were post offices in Dobbins, Downieville and Marysville. In 1852, Foster's Bar had a post office, and by 1855 there was one in Strawberry Valley and one in Oregon House.

8. *John Fall v. Wood* and *Scott, Vantine and Scott v. Wood* in Yuba County; *Flint v. Wood, McGlennon v. Wood, Corbett v. Wood* and *Doyle v. Wood* in Butte County.

9. The temperance movement later affected the sale of liquor, but not on a county-wide basis in either Yuba or Butte. Both Brownsville and Strawberry Valley adopted ordinances and for a while were "dry" towns.

10. The date that Joseph Wood left Woodville has long been a mystery. He told an interviewer for Thompson and West that he came to California in 1853, and to Yuba County in 1857, but that could have meant that he merely moved from one end of the hotel to the other. With the discovery of documents in the Yuba County Archives, unopened since 1858, his departure can be dated to within a period of about thirty-six days. The last record placing Joseph, Susan and Alice in Woodville is a hand-written document dated November 23, 1857, in which Wood verified that he had received an Order of Citation from Scott, Vantine and Company. Sometime between that date and December 30, he left Woodville.

11. John Abbott came to California in 1850 from Ohio, and lived for a time in Marysville, serving as Superintendent of Yuba County Schools until May of 1856. He sold the Lafayette Hotel in Forbestown after rebuilding it twice—in 1861 and 1862. In 1859-60 he was living in Oregon House and operating a hotel on Foster's Bar Road called the Oak Grove House. The

Woods settled nearby at Bell Valley. Family researchers believe that Abbott and Wood may have been distant relatives.

Susan R. Wood died March 9, 1869, at the age of forty-nine and the monument that marks her grave at the Keystone Cemetery in Oregon House reads, "As a wife, devoted; as a mother, affectionate; as a friend, ever kind and true." Within a few months of her death, Joseph sold the ranch, bought land near North San Juan and continued to enlarge his herds of fine horses. In 1870, when he was sixty-one, he married twenty-five-year-old Mary Elizabeth Young and fathered two sons, Charles and Joseph. He died February 1, 1889 at age 80, and is buried in the Protestant Cemetery in North San Juan. His grave marker reads, "Dear Husband and Father, how we miss you." His family still owns an ornate brass bed from the Woodville period, and wagons that are presently on loan to the State of California. His second wife, Elizabeth, lived until 1916; their son Charles died in 1952, and Joseph Jr. died in 1963.

The Wood family traces its beginnings in the United States to Nehemiah Wood, who arrived in Virginia in 1729, and their family tree includes many outstanding Americans, including former President Harry S. Truman. (See Lawler and Lawler.)

12. California Senate Bill #281, 1858, California State Archives; California State Law Library.

The Railroad Act of 1862 was passed in Congress and the Central Pacific Railroad began construction soon after. However, to Hangtown's sorrow, it did not follow the route of the National Wagon Road through the town. It began on the Pacific Coast and followed a more northerly route east to meet the Union Pacific, which originated in Omaha, Nebraska. The link was made in May 10, 1869, at Promontory Point, Utah.

13. A comprehensive story of John Rose's life was written by Diane Spencer-Pritchard (see bibliography) and covers many more details of his financial and commercial empire. (See also Yuba County Archives.)

14. The first fire occurred on January 28, 1860, with a loss of more than $30,000. After the business district had been rebuilt at great cost, it burned again on August 1, 1861, with a loss of more than $42,000. Two hotels, a drugstore, saloon, Masonic hall, meat market, restaurant, post office, shoe store, California Stage Company, Forbestown Brass Band, barbershop, water flumes owned by Wyandotte, China House, general mercantile shops, and the Tucker and Flint Saloon all were destroyed.

Among those who lost their buildings was Dr. William P. Flint, whose loss totaled more than $4,500. Lafayette Hotel, owned by J. M. Abbott, burned at a loss of $2,000. N. D. Plum and James Forbes, for whom Forbestown is named, lost $3,000 each when the United States Hotel burned. The townspeople did not give up and they rebuilt their town again.

15. Historians and architects differ in their interpretations of the hotel's style, but it resembles the Wood family home in Ohio. The most unique elements are the gabled parapets, i.e. walls projecting up at the ends of roof in the Georgian style. The Flemish Sweep or Dutch Kick, as the curved eaves are called, adorn the Woodleaf Hotel at the lower portion of the roof on the front of the building.

There have been numerous changes to the outside of the hotel. The dormers on the front and back were added around 1943, along with a low concrete wall with buttresses at the back, and a two-story addition on the northwest rear side. During the same time the original kitchen ell was torn down, the basement filled in, and the double doors closed in. Earlier changes were made by plastering the brick on the lower portions of the front and the entire back wall. The gabled parapets covered with clapboard siding are original, but in very poor condition, as are the four chimneys, which have lost much of their brick, and little of their design can be seen. The original posts and balusters were replaced during the late 1800s with flat, fancy-cut balusters, but fortunately these were later discarded and the elegantly simple ones restored. Most of the windows and the glass-paned, double doors with the low doorknobs are original. The 1968 replacement doors are quite different, with wide mullions between the glass panes and higher doorknobs. The original color of exterior paint was buff, trimmed in white. In 1968 the hotel was painted sage with white trim, a color also used during the 1850s in this area.

CHAPTER SEVEN
1. On February 28, 1861, Mr. De Long, State Senator from Butte County, introduced a bill to change the boundary line between the counties of Butte and Yuba at the Woodville House. It passed March 1, 1861, in the Senate, and on April 8, 1861, in the Assembly (California Senate, 12th Session, Bill #155).

Woodville was not the only property in the area that was affected by wandering county lines. In 1860, a law was passed enabling the entire town of Strawberry Valley to be in one county (Yuba). The towns of Clipper Mills and Forbestown remain partly in Butte, partly in Yuba.

The Butte and Yuba county assessors continued to disagree about Woodville when levying their taxes, since the property remained in both counties. The supervisors did not want to start another battle, however, and in 1897 convinced the state legislature to pass a new law, this time changing the county boundaries to correspond to the section lines so that all the Woodville property was in Yuba County, not just the Woodville Hotel. To avoid further trouble, they put the line one section beyond Woodville on each side.

2. The information on Charles Barker is sketchy. He was seriously injured in 1854 on his way to Sacramento when a stagecoach designed to carry fourteen passengers took on twenty-three people, most of them piled on top. The stage overturned, and most of the passengers were badly hurt. Barker had a broken hip and other injuries, and received $500 for his pains in a settlement with the California Stage Company. He apparently was unable to continue his trade as a house carpenter, joiner and contractor, and later operated the U.S. Stables in Marysville.

3. Herbert Young was a Maidu who lived near Feather Falls.

4. The family name originally was Canada, but it was changed to Kennedy. The exact date Nellie left Pakan'yani is unknown, but her son, John Kennedy, was born in Strawberry Valley in 1870, and her daughter, Elizabeth Johnson, was born in Nelson Point in 1872.

5. The diaries of G. S. W. Twogood record the period from 1873 to 1906 at Woodville, although the volumes for 1881-1890 are missing. Three of the entries about stage robberies are incidents involving Black Bart, and Twogood's information is verified by Wells Fargo records.

6. Information on this and other stagecoach robberies may be found in the Wells Fargo Archives, San Francisco.

CHAPTER EIGHT
1. Each town in the area had its own special day, celebrating one of the main holidays of the year. La Porte saluted Memorial Day with a big open-pit barbeque. In recent years, the crowds finally grew so large and disorderly that the town had to discontinue the long tradition. Woodleaf continued to host the 4th of July celebration until the 1940s.

2. In 1878, when Lotta was famous, she was still sentimental enough to want some part in the gold-mining business. She bought the Sawpit Mine near her childhood home, but the gold had been mined out of the claim, and it produced nothing, except perhaps memories.

A fountain erected in honor of Lotta Crabtree still stands in San Francisco. She died September 25, 1924, leaving an estate of nearly four million dollars. (See Dempsey.)

3. The Three Year Homestead Law of 1912 changed the residence requirement to three years. All such laws for acquiring U.S. land were later repealed.

Forbestown, Strawberry Valley, and Brownsville were formed under the Provisions for patenting townsites. Residents of Strawberry Valley patented the town land under the Townsite Act of 1884. The townsite was recorded in Yuba County and each person who met the requirements received a deed that transferred town property to them from the U.S. government. (See Robinson.)

4. James B. Kelly died in 1882, and in 1885 the property

was sold by his daughter, Maggie, to the Harter family, who later settled in Sutter County. Mrs. Kelly is somewhat of a mystery figure—she is mentioned briefly only once in Twogood's diaries, and no records of marriage, divorce or death have been found to date.

CHAPTER NINE

1. East of the Rockies, timber seldom reaches more than three feet in diameter. In contrast, the three major conifers growing in and around Woodleaf reach diameters of more than eight, twelve and fifteen feet and heights of two to three hundred feet. They are the ponderosa pine (*Pinus ponderosa*), sugar pine (*Pinus lambertiana*) and Douglas fir (*Pseudotsuga menziesii*), respectively. The Douglas fir is especially long-lived, and some have been found that are more than a thousand years old.

2. This first division is not recorded in county archives, but it is mentioned in a later document when Leach sold the store. Because the 1878 deed from Kelly to Falck specifically describes 160 acres, that sale obviously included the store and lot. The split thus took place between November 1878 and the date Leach sold the store: January 16, 1882. The first issue of *Woodleaf Legacy* and the Woodleaf section of the 1976 *Yuba County Bicentennial History* both were written before the discovery of the document that detailed this transaction, and err in stating that the first division in the history of the land occurred in the 1940s.

   Philip M. McDonald suggests that the survey of 1870 may have revealed that the mill at Woodville was just beyond Leach's boundaries, and that he might have purchased the 18.5 acres in a lot line adjustment. (For a comprehensive story of Leach, see McDonald and Lahore, p. 18-31.)

3. The tollhouse Twogood built is part of the Falck house today, the one-and-a-half-storey section on the northeast side. The old house that Twogood moved was located further northeast, and for many years was occupied by families working at Woodleaf. It was torn down in the early 1940s.

4. The grades of the track for Leach's narrow gauge railroad can still be followed south of Woodleaf along Indian Creek.

CHAPTER TEN

1. The information concerning Black Bart and Wells Fargo is from the Wells Fargo Archives, unless otherwise attributed.

2. The monument is located on Black Bart Road below Forbestown.

3. August (Gus) Robinson's recollection of meeting Charles Bolton at Woodville, courtesy of his daughter, Elizabeth Merian.

4. Agnes and Charles Falck, Helen and Jack Dunning and Florence Boyle described the letter in detail, and many people had seen it, along with his signature on the hotel register (as Bolton). Both documents were authenticated by a museum curator. After a visit from a collector during the 1930s, the letter, hotel register and other valuable documents disappeared.

5. Pacific Transcriptions, the publisher of Collins and Levene's *Black Bart* (1992), is one of the latest to offer "$1,000 REWARD . . . to the first person who can provide, to us exclusively, indisputable proof of the date of death and place of death of Charles E. Boles, otherwise known as Black Bart."

6. According to the Falcks, Grant's signature also appeared in the hotel register. Tradition holds that Ulysses S. Grant also stayed at one of the hotels in Marysville on his tour through the West. The U.S. had problems raising money for the Civil War debts, and in 1866 Congress proposed selling mineral lands in the West, but this was promptly quashed.

CHAPTER ELEVEN

1. The Congressional Act of July 25, 1866, granted U.S. lands to the railroad to help with the enormous construction costs. The vacant, odd-numbered sections, twenty to thirty miles on each side of a railroad line, could be claimed by the railroad companies. In return, the U.S. received free use of the railroad for mail service and lower rates for government traffic. By the end of World War II, the rate reductions for all railroads in the U.S. reached a total of one billion dollars, more than eight times the value of the lands at the time they were granted to the railroads. The lands that were not used were sold when the railroad was finished, and a patent was issued from the United States Land Office to each new owner. The amount of land sold was so vast—many millions of acres—that the government office was swamped. Some new owners had to wait twenty years before their railroad sale was processed and they received their deed. It would be only eighteen years for the Falcks—twenty-three days after John Falck died in 1901 they received their deed to the land.

2. In 1881, the court ruled against the mining company in the case of *The People v. Gold Run Mining Company*, yet the company continued hydraulic mining without pause. A U.S. Circuit Court decision in 1884 ruled hydraulic mining legal, but declared that it was illegal to dump debris into state waters. After many more battles, the Caminetti Act, supported by miners, was adopted in 1893, giving the California Debris Commission supervision over hydraulic mining. Ironically, the Commission demanded the building of debris dams that were so expensive that hydraulic mining died almost overnight. Only a few were financially sound enough to construct debris dams, and they continued operating into the 1940s.

3. In the 1950s, houses, shops and barns still stood in many of these towns, street upon street, some leaning haphazardly from the thirty-foot snows of winter, some with their windows boarded up, many with all the fur-

nishings intact. The old Marysville-La Porte stage stood covered with dust in a barn, unmoved for decades. Many buildings were later vandalized, others burned or rotted away, and a few were claimed as mining property and repaired. The La Porte stage is now owned by Knotts Berry Farm in southern California, where it was restored and is ridden by tourists.

4. Leach was born in Pittsford, Vermont, on December 7, 1841, and came to California sometime prior to 1873. After his lumbering empire collapsed, Leach moved to Dunsmuir in 1894 and began building homes and apartments, a very successful enterprise. He died on Christmas day in 1908 (McDonald and Lahore, pp. 18-31).

5. By the time Maude Hill wrote her story, the town's name had been changed and she used the new name. For the sake of clarity, "Woodleaf" is replaced with "Woodville," in this text.

6. The Yuba County Tax Assessment, December 29, 1890, lists a two-story brick house-$2,000, barn-$300, fence-$150, watch-$100, furniture-$485, piano-$150, sewing machine-$20, kitchen utensils-$30, two wagons-$100, two horses-$150, two cows-$35, hogs-$10, 192 acres-$300. Total value, $3,830; tax, $76.40 (Yuba County Archives).

7. These baskets were later donated to the Plumas County Museum in Quincy by Sophia's grandson, Lawrence Falck. One basket, which bears the words "Mrs. J. S. Kennedy, Plumas County," woven into the design, is believed to have been made by Nellie's daughter-in-law, Sarah Kennedy, wife of John Kennedy.

8. The store changed hands several times: from Leach to Thomas Parsons, to Rachel Bradley, then finally to Falck.

9. Agnes Riker's family came from the Bay Area. Her brother founded a religious group at Holy City in the Santa Cruz mountains west of Los Gatos, and was known as Father Riker.

CHAPTER TWELVE

1. Beginning around 1896, Twogood moved to Brownsville each winter to operate the family store and work as Brownsville postmaster. During the summers, his wife took over his duties at the post office, and he moved back to Woodville to work as the tollkeeper.

2. Lizzie was Twogood's daughter, and Lawrence was the newest member of the Falck family; both were born at Woodleaf.

3. Ruff Hill in Brownsville is named for the Ruff family.

4. Twogood became a deputy assessor for Yuba County, walking over many miles of property, and continued to work as postmaster and storekeeper in Brownsville until 1909. He was seventy-nine years old when he and Susan moved to Chico to live near their family. He died at age eighty-three, March 30, 1912. Susan lived to be eighty-one, and died in 1922.

5. Arbucco had several mines in the vicinity, and also the Challenge Quartz Claim on Crane's Creek in Challenge. Some of the mine shafts remain open and the surface is overgrown with brush, making it dangerous to hike in the area. In the 1950s, the notices of the claims were still mounted on pieces of wood, nailed to trees.

6. The Colgate power plant, built on the Yuba River in 1899, was in the process of being expanded. This plant utilized a system of flumes and ditches originally built for mining, and a supplemental dam at Lake Francis in Dobbins, to provide electricity to Sacramento and to the gold dredgers in Oroville—the state's first long-distance transmission of power to valley cities. Throughout the Sierras, hydro-electric companies took over water rights and the vast systems of flumes, dams and ditches, using them to produce electricity.

7. Agnes Falck remodeled the family home during the 1950s, installing modern aluminum frame windows, asbestos siding and removing the ornate staircase in the front hall. She built a separate entry and stairway at the back of the house so that she and her children's families could share the home, but have private entries and living quarters.

8. During repairs to the hotel in 1969, the broken pieces of an ornate porcelain water closet of very early manufacture were found beneath the hotel. It may have been damaged when the ceiling collapsed.

   Sophia Hedstrom Falck died October 3, 1912, and is buried at the Strawberry Valley Cemetery.

9. Alex Picayune was born November 14, 1879, in Butte County. According to a 1969 interview with Herbert Young (courtesy of Dorothy J. Hill), the Picayune family once lived near Feather Falls, and their ancestors founded one of the Maidu settlements.

10. Keith paid the back taxes on the property before deeding it to the United States on May 24, 1918. The land is described in letters as part of the 320 acres patented in trust for the townsite of Strawberry Valley and formerly owned by David E. Berry (Lot 12, Block B in Strawberry Valley Townsite).

11. The official name for this land parcel was Strawberry Valley Rancheria. The eighty-acre Picayune Rancheria in Madera County was occupied by the Yokuts Indians, not related to Alex Picayune. Most Indian parcels were larger, some of them many thousands of acres, especially in other states. In California the grants ranged from the smallest at Strawberry Valley, to 49,000 acres, the largest, at Hoopa Valley. (See Garcia.)

12. Information about Nellie and her family was obtained from her descendants, some still living in the area, and from documents listed in the bibliography.

    In 1924, legislation was passed granting United States citizenship to native peoples, conferring the rights so long denied them, including the right to own land and vote.

Nellie lived on the Maidu land in Strawberry Valley until her death on January 11, 1937. She is buried in Sierra View Cemetery in Marysville. Alex and Elizabeth Picayune and their son, Clifford, and daughter, Nellie Frances Williams Picayune, also lived on the tribal property until their deaths. Alex Picayune died March 23, 1959; his wife, Elizabeth, in 1942. Their son, Clifford, who served in World War II, died April 7, 1949. Nellie Frances Williams was adopted by Alex Picayune when he married Elizabeth. She died at age twenty of pneumonia in Strawberry Valley in 1920.

In 1958, the group's status as a tribe was terminated by the California Rancheria Act (PL85-671). This act affected many tribes, including those at the Mooretown Rancheria near Feather Falls. Their status as Indians was ended, and their land was deeded to families remaining in the group. The Strawberry Valley land was deeded in 1959 to Nellie's granddaughter, Sophia Wyman, who was living in Berry Creek, and she eventually sold it. It is no longer Maidu land.

Mooretown Rancheria was re-established after *Tillie Hardwick v. United States* was won in 1983, which recognized the Maidu/Concow tribe and sixteen other tribes. Since that time, the Maidu/Concow tribe has gathered more than five hundred members, organized a tribal council, and purchased land in Butte County. Descendants of Nellie belong to this tribe.

CHAPTER THIRTEEN

1. Both the Oroville-La Porte and Marysville-La Porte stages were owned by the Pauley brothers in 1914. The drivers of the Marysville-La Porte stage, Dan Boland and Terry Reilly, switched to driving the new vehicles (weather permitting) (Gould, p. 42). The line retained the name "Marysville-La Porte Stage," however, and passengers regularly rode the route well into the late fifties. The mail truck is still known as the "stage." In 1930 Elizabeth Merian bought the contract from the Pauly brothers, becoming the line's first woman stage driver.

2. This article was one of a series which ran in the newspaper, decrying the condition of all the county roads.

3. The radio may have operated with the enormous batteries of the time, or used electricity from the large diesel generator that provided power for the hotel and store at Woodleaf. Despite the flourishing tourist trade, electricity from a public utility company had not reached any of the small towns in this part of the Sierra. Strawberry Valley had a large diesel generator that produced power for the hotel, beginning around 1913. Lloyd Silva of Strawberry Valley was often called upon to repair it. Challenge also used a generator for power for its hotels and stores, but homes and cottages remained without electricity. Perhaps the tourists found lamplight in the cottages quaint and appealing (Lloyd Silva, Jack Dunning, interviews).

4. The school year in mountain towns ran from March

to September, or sometimes October, because of the heavy snows in winter. It was nearly impossible to travel with any regularity to the schoolhouse to keep the doors, windows, roof and chimney shoveled off, pathways cleared, and firewood in stock.

5. When the Prohibition Amendment was repealed in 1933, liquor was again sold in the bar—legally.

6. Helen Falck Dunning and Jack Dunning were the source of many stories about life in Woodleaf. They had an unerring memory for dates and names; details were confirmed time after time by newspapers, county records and diaries. Jack died in 1982 and Helen in 1991.

CHAPTER FOURTEEN

1. The deed was signed January 5, 1943; the purchase price $15,000. Some land in the area was selling for $10-$35 per acre, so it was a good price for the 180 acres with buildings. In spite of low prices, there were few buyers. Jobs were scarce and banks would not lend on land in this area, considering it worthless.

The Falcks kept the two houses that are presently known as the Roadhouse and the Falck House. They also retained lot numbers 69, 70, 71, 72 and 73 of Woodleaf Lodge Subdivision until October 18, 1950, when they sold them to Sacramento Box and Lumber Company. Charles Falck died in 1948; Agnes in 1967.

2. A small, temporary mill was installed at the top of Barton Hill to cut most of the construction timber and lumber for the Woodleaf mill.

3. The back porch and kitchen "ell" on the Hotel, built in 1857, were torn down and the cellar filled in. Three dormers were added to the hotel roof in back and one in front to bring in light. A two-story addition was built onto the back, outfitted with showers and restrooms.

4. There was a waiting list of families who wanted to move to Woodleaf, and it sometimes took years for a house to become available. Some employees commuted from Oroville and Marysville to work each day, preferring to raise their families in town where schools, churches, medical facilities and shopping were nearby. Many employees maintained homes in small towns surrounding Woodleaf. The four large houses were occupied by the Yard, Woods, and Mill superintendents, the General Manager and their families.

Besides the pre-cut houses, Burke traded lumber for other goods and equipment that were under rationing. Tires, fuel, oil, steel machine parts, cable and numerous other supplies were all necessary to operate the mill.

5. Dottie Duggan Kearns was the daughter of an employee of Sacramento Box and her mother, Hazel, was postmaster at Woodleaf. The Duggan family, along with the Damon family, were the first to move to Woodleaf after Sacramento Box and Lumber Company constructed the homes.

6. Besides approximately seventeen million board feet in

the log deck next to the pond, an additional seventeen to twenty-one million board feet was decked on the hill above the pond with a separate high-line operation.

The mill operated year round except for one or two weeks after Christmas, when it shut down for repairs. From May to November, the mill ran two shifts, one from 7:30 a.m. to 4:30 p.m.; another 4:30 p.m. to 2:30 a.m. From November to May it operated days only.

7. E. F. Muster was involved in employee-company relations as the president of the union, and recalls that Mr. Burke was held in very high regard by employees and management alike.

8. The landslide was thought to have been caused by a road that was cut through the hillside to gain access to timber in the adjoining section of land. Geologists had advised against disturbing the area, which was composed of unstable clay and serpentine, and had several springs.

9. There were five additional schools in the surrounding area—Strawberry Valley, Clipper Mills, Sharon Valley (Brownsville), Hansonville (Rackerby) and Forbestown. Two other schools in the area had been discontinued: Greenville School on Oregon Hill Road, and Empire School. The six schools eventually combined into the Yuba Feather School District, and in 1952 built a large school in Challenge.

10. Strawberry Valley, Challenge and Brownsville students went Marysville High School, since they were in Yuba County; Clipper Mills and Forbestown students living in Butte County attended Oroville High School.

11. The bell was purchased by church members from Alex Moran of Challenge, and originally came from the Greenville School on Oregon Hill Road.

12. A few artifacts were salvaged, such as the safe and a butcher's meat scale, which are on display in the town today. The northeast end of the lower floor of the hotel was set up as a temporary store and the post office moved in with it. Later, a butcher shop and barber shop opened in the hotel.

13. Capacity according to Carl Sundahl, former Yard Manager. A bronze plaque that the builders mounted on the finished construction is displayed in the hotel in Woodleaf.

14. William E. Sundahl is a son of Carl and Myrtle Sundahl, and lived in Woodleaf during the mill years.

CHAPTER FIFTEEN

1. This organization is best described in one of its publications. "Young Life was founded by Jim Rayburn, a seminary student in Texas who wanted to reach out to young people who seemed disinterested in God and the church. Today the mission is still committed to embodying and expressing the love of Christ in relationships with people. . . . In 1990, there were 600 full-time staff, and over 12,000 volunteers working with young people" (*Young Life*, p. 1).

2. Since Woodleaf was purchased in 1966, Young Life has acquired more properties to serve its growing numbers. In 1953 the first international work began, and is now continuing in thirty-eight countries.

3. Shortly after scouting out the Woodleaf property, Mitchell joined the staff at Young Life's international headquarters in Colorado Springs, and Bob Reeverts was named Western Regional Director in Palo Alto. The Woodleaf development office was also located in Palo Alto.

4. A California corporation working with the U.S. Peace Corps negotiated the short-term lease for Woodleaf.

5. In the first year of Young Life's ownership, the four large homes, formerly used by mill supervisors, were set up as: 1) resident caretaker; 2) ladies' bunkhouse; 3) men's bunkhouse, combined with the camp kitchen and staff dining room; 4) meeting house. The staff family who later moved into the "kitchen-dining room-bunkroom" on the hill found two huge cookstoves, seven bunkbeds, ten tables, thirty chairs, a well-beaten path to the roadway, and a bathtub worn down to the bare metal.

During the mill years, residents had added bedrooms to some of the houses and finished small basement rooms. The extra bedrooms remain, for the most part. Young Life staff used the basement rooms and individual garages for storage and shops until the shop facility was built in 1990 ("Old Bill's"). The carpentry, plumbing, mechanical, metalwork, and groundskeeping shops are combined, forming the headquarters of the Woodleaf work force. The outdoor decks, porches, arbors, fences and patios of individual homes, constructed during the mill years, gradually deteriorated and only a few remain.

6. The dining room and kitchen were remodeled and extended many times: 1968, 1970, 1974, and 1977-78. The last renovation moved the dining hall entry to face the meadow, and revamped the old hall for summer staff housing.

Before Young Life purchased Woodleaf, the old saloon's massive, slate-topped pool tables with carved wooden legs and trim were sold for $25 each. The wooden score rings and pool cue rack remain at Woodleaf.

The store was called "Trading Post" for a brief time in the summer of 1968, but this was quickly dropped because it was not appropriate to the town's history. There were no trading posts in this area even during the time of the fur trappers. As early as 1850 a "store" was in operation on the property, and one has been in business almost continuously since that time. The name was changed back to "Woodleaf Store" in the fall of 1968.

The Town Hall was remodeled several times before Young Life's ownership, and in 1968, 1970, and 1989.

7. Bob Wagner, a Maidu man who lives in the vicinity, hand-split the posts and rails and installed them. Today, at age ninety, he no longer works with wood,

but teaches the younger generations his craft.

8. Woodleaf is located on the divide between the Feather and Yuba rivers. The rain and snow that falls at the front of the hotel belong to the Yuba River watershed; at the back, to the Feather River watershed. Special permits were obtained during the mill years to bring water from one watershed to the other.

9. The Roadhouse was originally a small summer cottage, enlarged during the late 1940s with material from Beale Air Force Base.

10. The original land claim of 160 acres, plus the forty acres of railroad land, was intact, except, of course, for the 18.5 acres that had reverted to the U.S. government after the demise of the Woodville Steam Sawmill in 1887.

    The Falck House exterior was refurbished in 1973. Old photographs were studied with a magnifying glass to determine the design of porch rails, lattice and shutters, and the replacement balusters were cut by hand. The original wood siding was found to be in good condition beneath the asbestos siding. Remnants of the original paint showed that the house had been painted yellow ochre, and the new color was matched to the old. The original trim was dark maroon or brown and the second coat was white, the color used in the renovation. New shutters were put in place, but it was not possible at the time to replace the aluminum windows or restore the interior of the house.

11. The six resident boxholders in 1971 were: Young Life (Office), William Ingersoll, Richard Schroeder, John and Christine Lundin, Mossinger family, and Bill Styles. The Woodleaf zip code, 95990, was retired and has not been re-assigned.

    Bill Styles, along with another elderly man, Hank Norblade, were promised a place to stay after the mill closed. All the homes and cottages in that section of town had previously burned or were torn down, and these men occupied small cabins, and paid no rent. Hank Norblade was employed by Sacramento Box at Kyburz, and moved to Woodleaf in 1942, working there until the mill closed in 1965. He died in January, 1969, electrocuted by a power line that fell during a storm. Bill Styles was not employed by the company, but was offered a place to stay after his cabin, which was several miles away, burned around 1961. He left Woodleaf in 1979, and lived in Sacramento until his death on March 25, 1986, at age 99.

12. Dennis Woll, Woodleaf property manager since 1992, today works with the staff that includes Wes Owen, Pete Haney, Wayne Wright, Brian Kyte, Brad Hudson, Norm Jones, Jani Blakemore, Valerie O'Rourke, Bev Owen, Lisa Boyd, Donna Holmes, Pat Schermerhorn, Chris Babb, Heather Darnell, Tammy Thorpe, Jean Bettin and Susan Bell.

13. Jack Murtha developed the school in the early 1960s, and was joined by Bob Jacoby in 1966, working through the office of Sutter County Superintendent of Schools. Sites at Butte Meadows and Bear Valley were utilized prior to 1969.

    In addition to the Young Life Woodleaf property, a study area was developed in 1969 in cooperation with the U.S. Forest Service, at Kellogg Flat (site of the Erastus Kellogg homestead that was never patented). This was discontinued when the program obtained access to land closer to Woodleaf through a special use permit with the U.S. Forest Service.

14. Woodleaf Outdoor Education Foundation is a nonprofit corporation dedicated to raising funds for the outdoor school. Inquiries may be directed to 146 Garden Highway, Yuba City, California, 95991.

15. John Hendrickson is a noted wildlife photographer whose work has appeared in *National Geographic*, *Audubon*, *Newsweek*, and numerous other publications. His book, *Raptors: Birds of Prey*, was published in 1992 by Chronicle Books, San Francisco.

16. Most of the trees in logging areas are cut while fairly small, i.e., two to three feet in diameter, and few are left to grow to their full size. The term, "mature timber," describes a relatively young tree that may be profitably harvested. It does not mean that the tree is old or will soon die. In California, conifers will continue to grow hundreds of years and can reach massive proportions of eight to ten and even fifteen feet in diameter, as related in Chapter Nine and Note 9:1. These magnificent giants are rarely seen today except in specially preserved groves.

For more information concerning the current operation of Woodleaf, or to arrange a visit, please contact the business office:

Young Life Woodleaf
P.O. Box 397
Challenge, California 95925
916-675-2252

Bibliography

Bancroft, Hubert Howe, *History of California,* San Francisco History Company, 1888. Vol. VI, 1848-59.

————, *Native Races of Pacific States,* 5 vols., 1875.

Bartlett, J. R., *Personal Narrative of Explorations and Incidents Connected with the United States and Mexican Boundary Commission,* 1854.

Berry, Thomas Senior, *Early California Gold Prices and Trade,* University of Richmond, Bostwick Press, 1984.

Bosshard, R. E., *Pony Express Courier,* Alameda, California, 1941.

Brown, W. C., *Marysville Directory,* 1861 and 1862.

Browne, J. Ross, *A Peep at Washoe,* Biobooks, Palo Alto, California, 1968.

————, *Crusoe's Island—With Sketches of Adventures in California,* Sampson, Low, Son and Marston, 1864.

————, *Illustrated Mining Adventures in California and Nevada, 1863-1865,* Paisano Press, Balboa Island, California, 1961.

————, *Indians of California,* Colt Press, San Francisco, 1944.

————, *Western Panorama, 1849-1875,* A. H. Clark, Glendale, California, 1966.

Buffum, Edward Gould, *Six Months in the Gold Mines,* Lea and Blanchard, 1966.

California State Publications, *Journal of the Twelfth Session, California State Legislature,* 1861.

Calliet, Emile, *Young Life,* Young Life, Colorado Springs, 1963.

Chittenden, H. M., *Fur Trade of the Far West,* Press of the Pioneers, New York, 1935.

Coleman, Charles M., *P. G. and E. of California,* 1852-1952, McGraw-Hill, Inc., New York, 1952.

Colville, Samuel, *Marysville Directory,* 1855-1856.

Collins, William, and Bruce Levene, *Black Bart: The True Story of the West's Most Famous Stagecoach Robber,* Pacific Transcriptions, Mendocino, California, 1992.

Cook, Sherbourne C., *Population of California Indians, 1769-1970,* University of California Press, 1976.

Cordua, Theodor, *Memoirs of Theodor Cordua,* Erwin G. Gudde, ed. and trans., Quarterly of California Historical Society, Vol. XII, No. 4 (December, 1933).

Coy, Owen C., *California County Boundaries,* California Historical Survey Commission, Berkeley, 1923.

De Lay, Peter J., *History of Yuba and Sutter Counties,* Historic Record Company, Los Angeles, 1924.

Delano, Alonzo, *Life on the Plains and Among the Diggings,* Wilson Erickson, Inc., New York, 1936.

Dempsey, David, and Raymond P. Baldwin, *The Triumphs and Trials of Lotta Crabtree,* William Morrow and Company, Inc., New York, 1968.

Dixon, Roland B., *The Northern Maidu,* The Huntington California Expedition, Bulletin of the American Museum of Natural History, New York, 1905.

Downie, Major William, *Hunting for Gold,* California Publishing Company, San Francisco, 1893.

Farris-Smith, *History of Plumas, Lassen and Sierra Counties,* 1882.

Forbes, Jack, *Native Americans of California and Nevada,* Naturegraph Publishing Company, Healdsburg, California, 1969.

Garcia, Jesse, *Location and Character of Indian Lands in California,* Phillip J. Webster and Staff, United States Department of Agriculture, 1937.

Gould, Helen Weaver, *La Porte Scrapbook,* Gould, La Porte, 1972.

Gudde, Erwin G., *Bigler's Chronicle of the West,* University of California Press, Berkeley, 1962.

Heizer, Robert F., *Languages, Territories and Names of California Indian Tribes,* University of California Press, Berkeley and Los Angeles, 1966.

————, *The Destruction of California Indians,* 1847-1865, Peregrine Smith, Inc., Santa Barbara, 1974.

Hill, Dorothy, *Maidu Use of Native Flora and Fauna,* Chico State University, Chico, California, 1968.

Hill, Maude Gilbert, "Turn of the Wheel," *Butte Remembers,* Butte County Historical Society,

1973.

Jewell, Donald P., *Indians of the Feather River*, Ballena Press, Menlo Park, California, 1987.

Knapp, Louise Amelia (1819-1906), *The Shirley Letters*, Grabhorn Press, 1933.

Kroeber, A. L., *Handbook of the Indians of California*, University of California, Bureau of American Ethnology of the Smithsonian Institution, Bulletin 78, 1925.

Lawler, Leo G., and Hazel P. Lawler, *Nehemiah Wood of Shenandoah County, Virginia,* Fredericksburg, Virginia, 1980.

Lewis, Henry T., *Patterns of Indian Burning in California: Ecology and Ethnohistory*, Ballena Press, Menlo Park, California, 1973.

Lightner, Otto C., *History of Business Depressions*, B. Franklin, New York, 1970.

Loomis, Noel M., *Wells Fargo*, Clarkson N. Potter, Inc., New York, 1968.

Mansfield, George C., *History of Butte County*, Historic Records Company, Los Angeles, 1918.

McDonald, Philip M., and Lona F. Lahore, "Lumbering in the Northern Sierra Nevada: Andrew Martin Leach of Challenge Mills," *The Pacific Historian*, Vol. 28, No. 2 (Summer 1984), University of the Pacific, Stockton, California.

McKenney and Co., *City and County Directory of Yuba, Sutter, Colusa, Butte, Tehama Counties,* 1881.

Merriam, C. Hart, *Reports of the University of California Archaeological Survey, No. 68, Part III*, Robert F. Heizer, ed., Department of Anthropology, Berkeley, December, 1967.

Morrell, W. P., *The Gold Rushes*, University of London, Macmillan Company, New York, 1941.

Muir, John, "A Wind Storm in the Forests of the Yuba," *Scribner's Monthly*, 1878.

Newhouse, Sewell, *The Trapper's Guide,* Oneida, New York, 1800s.

Peterson, Lee Allen, *Edible Wild Plants*, Houghton Mifflin Company, Boston, 1977.

Petrides, George A. and Olivia, *Western Trees,* Houghton Mifflin Company, New York, 1992.

Potts, Marie Gould, *The Northern Maidu*, Naturegraph Publishers, Inc., Happy Camp, California, 1977.

Powell, J. W., *Indian Land Cessions in the United States*, 18th Annual Report of the Bureau of American Ethnology, Smithsonian Institution, Washington, D.C., 1899.

Powers, Stephen, *The Northern California Indians*, 19 articles originally published 1872-1877, Robert F. Heizer, ed., University of California, Department of Anthropology, Berkeley, 1975.

————, *Tribes of California*, Department of the Interior, U.S. Geological Survey, 1877.

Riddell, Francis A., "Maidu and Konkow," *Handbook of North American Indians*, Vol. 8, Smithsonian Institution, 1978.

Robinson, W. W., *Land in California*, University of California Press, Berkeley, 1948.

Shipley, William F., *Maidu Texts and Dictionary*, University of California Press, Berkeley, 1963.

Shipley, William F., and Richard A. Smith, "The Roles of Cognation and Diffusion in a Theory of Maidu Prehistory," *Journal of California and Great Basin Anthropology*, 1979.

Smith, Mix, and G. Amy, *Marysville Directory*, 1858-1859.

Spencer-Pritchard, Diane, "Gold Rush Gambler: Yuba County's John Rose," *The Californians*, July/August 1990, pp. 18-24.

Stillman, Jacob D. B., *The Gold Rush Letters of Jacob D. B. Stillman*, Kenneth Johnson, ed., Palo Alto, California, 1967.

Sundahl, William E., *A Glimpse of Woodleaf and the Forbestown Road in the 1940s*, Yuba Feather Historical Museum, Booklet #4, 1994.

Swanton, John R., *Indian Tribes of North America*, Smithsonian Institution, Bureau of American Ethnology, Bulletin 145, U.S. Printing Office, Washington, D.C., 1952.

Taylor, Bayard, *El Dorado*, New York and London, 1850.

Thompson and West, *History of Yuba County*, 1879.

Wells and Chambers, *History of Butte County*, 1882.

Wilkes, Captain Charles, *Columbia River to the Sacramento, 1839-1842*, Biobooks, Oakland, 1958.

Wilkeson, Samuel, *Notes on the Reconnaissance of Proposed Route of the NPRR,* 1869.

Work, John, *Fur Brigade to the Bonaventura*, John

Work's California Expedition 1832-1833 for the Hudson's Bay Company, Alice Bay Maloney, ed., San Francisco Historical Society, San Francisco, 1945.

Young Life: Remembering Fifty Years of Serving Christ and Kids, 1940-1990, Young Life Campaign, Colorado Springs, Colorado, 1990.

Yuba County, *Directory of Yuba County,* 1903-04.

UNPUBLISHED MATERIAL

Adams, C. F., diaries, private collection.

Adams, Erma, diaries, private collection.

Bartholomew, J., diaries, Lilly Library, University of Indiana, Bloomington, Indiana.

Bigler, Henry, diary, Society of California Pioneers, San Francisco.

Boles, Charles, letter, Earl Bowles, Redwood, New York.

Bustillos, Jesus, "Daybook of Jesus Bustillos," Bancroft Library, Berkeley.

Dick Hadley Real Estate brochure, 1965, private collection.

Kowta, Makoto, "The Archaeology and Prehistory of Plumas and Butte Counties, California: An Introduction and Interpretive Model," Chico State University, Chico, California, 1988.

Manter, J. A., letter to Hiram Manter, private collection.

McGowan, Joseph Aloysius, "Freighting to the Mines of California 1848-1859," Bancroft Library, Berkeley, 1949.

Morse, E. W., diaries, Huntington Library, San Marino, California.

Mossinger journals, private collection.

Parke, Charles, journal, Huntington Library, San Marino, California.

Organ, William J., journal, private collection.

Pratt, J. W., letter, May, 1879, Thompson and West Collection, Huntington Library, San Marino, California.

Spect, Jonas, letter, 1879, Thompson and West Collection, Huntington Library, San Marino, California.

Swain, William, diaries, Yale University, Coe Collection, New Haven, Connecticut.

Twogood, G. S. W., diaries, private collection.

NEWSPAPERS & PERIODICALS

Alta California Press, 1850

Ballou's Pictorial Drawing Room Companion, 1857

Banner, 1867-1880

Butte Record, up to 1880

California Express, 1851-1863

California Star, 1848

California Transcript, 1850

Century Magazine

Daily Butte Record

Gold Mountain Record, 1975-1993

Harper's Weekly, 1875-77

Harper's New Monthly Magazine, 1860-1865

Hutchings' California Magazine, 1859, 1860

Marysville Appeal Democrat, 1940-present

Marysville Appeal Directory, 1878-1879

Marysville Daily Appeal, 1860-1867; 1883-1909?

Marysville Daily News, 1858

Marysville Daily Democrat, 1884-1909

Marysville Daily National Democrat, 1858-1861

Marysville Democrat, 1923

Marysville Evening Democrat, 1910-1923

Marysville Herald, 1850-1858

Marysville Star, 1835-1836

Marysville Weekly Appeal, 1864-1882, 1889

Missouri Republican, 1827

Mountain Messenger

North Californian (Oroville)

Oroville Register, 1880-1927

Oroville Mercury, 1927-present

Oroville Union Record

Placer Times, June 17, 1850

Sacramento Placer Times, 1849-1850

Sacramento Transcript, April 1, 1850-March 29, 1851

Sacramento Union, 1852

Sacramento Bee, 1952

San Francisco Call, 1883 and 1888

San Francisco Chronicle, 1883 and 1888

Scribner's Monthly, 1878

Splinters, 1940s-50s

MAPS

Butte County, 1862, Bancroft Library, University of California, Berkeley

Feather and Yuba Rivers, (Eddy) 1851, Bancroft Library, University of California, Berkeley

Sacramento Box and Lumber Company, c. 1953, Young Life, Woodleaf, California

Sacramento Valley, 1849, General Riley, RG77, Records of the Chief Engineer, File W-10, National Archives, Washington, D.C.

Turnpike Survey, 1853, California State Archives, Sacramento

U.S. Geological Survey, 1948, Plumas National Forest, Quincy, California

Woodleaf Subdivision, 1929, Yuba County Archives, Marysville, California

Woodleaf Topographic and Boundary Map, 1987, Young Life, Woodleaf, California

Yuba County, 1861, 1887, 1909, 1939, 1953, California State Library, Sacramento

Yuba County Assessor's Maps, 1962, 1991, Yuba County Archives, Marysville, California

Yuba County Road Maps, Yuba County Public Works, Marysville, California

PERSONAL COMMUNICATIONS

Charles "Bud" Adams, Andrew Arbucco, Florence Boyle, Roy Brown, P. V. Burke, Mary Wood Calvert, Mabel Wood Carr, Don Cosens, Marge Cosens, Helen Falck Dunning, Jack Dunning, Ben Falck, Agnes Riker Falck, Charles Lawrence Falck, Lawrence Falck, Jann Garvis, John Hendrickson, Dorothy J. Hill, Bill Holmes, Marge Holmes, Pearl Logan, Virgil Logan, Edwin Magruder, Elizabeth Merian, Philip McDonald, Bob Moller, Lorraine Mullins Frazier, E. F. Muster, Wilhelmina Muster, Bill Prater, Sandra Dunning Noel, Lloyd Silva, Carl Sundahl, G. J. Thompson, Zelma Wood Skoog, Dennis Woll.

LIBRARIES AND ARCHIVES

Bancroft Library, Berkeley, California:
    Diaries, Documents, Maps, Photographs

Butte County Archives, Oroville and Chico, California:
    Assessments, 15th District Court Minute Book, Births, Book of Lis Pendens 1855-1859, Deaths, Deeds, Great Register of Voters 1866-1909, Homesteads, Judgment Docket 1851-1879, Licenses, Marriages, Mechanic's Liens, Mining Claims, Miscellaneous Records, Pre-emptions, Probate, Surveys

California State Law Library, Sacramento, California

California Society of Pioneers, San Francisco, California

California State Library, Sacramento, California:
    California State Special Census 1852, Photographs, Louis Stellman Collection, Maps, Survey Records, U.S. Census Records

Chico University, Special Collections, Meriam Library, Chico, California

De Young Museum, San Francisco, California

Huntington Library, San Marino, California, Thompson and West Collection

Lilly Library, Indiana University, Bloomington, Indiana, J. Bartholomew Collection

National Archives, Washington, D.C.:
    Indian Rolls of 1928, Correspondence, Rancherias, Land Allotments

Plumas County Museum, Quincy, California, C. L. Falck Collection

Siskiyou County Museum, Yreka, California

Smithsonian Institution, Washington, D.C.

Society of California Pioneers, San Francisco, California

United States Bureau of Land Management, Sacramento, California:
    U.S. Land Claims, Pre-emptions, Patents

United States Post Office:
    Applications, Establishment of Post Offices, Postmaster Appointments, Site Records, Discontinuance Records

Wells Fargo Archives, Wells Fargo Bank, San Francisco, California

Yale University, Coe Collection, New Haven, Connecticut.

Yuba County Archives, Marysville, California:
    10th District Court Files, Assessments, Births, Deaths, Deeds, Great Register of Yuba County, Gold Mining Poll Tax Register, Homesteads, Justice of the Peace Records, Licenses, Marriages, Mining Claims, Miscellaneous Records, Mortgages, Pre-emptions, Supervisor's Proceedings, Survey Records

Text Credits

Quotations in this book appear through the courtesy of the following institutions, collections and individuals, and from the following interviews and publications:
1, 2—Epigraph and text: Shipley, *Maidu Texts and Dictionary,* pp. 79, 81; 5, 7—Potts, *The Northern Maidu,* pp. 14-16, 45-46, Naturegraph Publishing Company; 11—Epigraph: Smith quote, *Missouri Republican,* October 11, 1827; 12—Work, *Fur Brigade to the Bonaventura,* pp. iii, iv, 28, California Historical Society; 13—Caption: Miller quote, Walters Art Gallery; Wilkes, *Columbia River to the Sacramento, 1839-1842,* p. 349; 14-16—Work, *Fur Brigade to the Bonaventura;* 17—Thompson and West, *History of Yuba County,* p. 24; 18—Work, *Fur Brigade to the Bonaventura;* 21—Epigraph: Gudde, *Bigler's Chronicle of the West;* Cordua, *Memoirs of Theodor Cordua,* p. 17; *California Star,* May 20, 1848; Spect quote, The Huntington Library; 22—Manter quote, Kirk Wolford; 22, 23—Downie, *Hunting for Gold,* p. 126; 23—Mooney quote, Thompson and West, *History of Yuba County,* p. 83; 26—Downie, *Hunting for Gold,* p. 25; 27—Organ, p. 44, Kathe Goria-Hendrickson; 29—Downie, *Hunting for Gold,* pp. 21, 22; 31—Stillman, *Goldrush Letters of Jacob Stillman;* 32—Buffum, *Six Months in the Gold Mines,* p. 62; 33—Twogood quote, Louis E. Edwards; 35—Epigraph and text: *Placer Times,* June 17, 1850; Organ, p. 51, Kathe Goria-Hendrickson; Thompson and West, *History of Yuba County,* p. 43; *Placer Times,* June 17, 1850; 36, 37—Downie, *Hunting for Gold,* p. 176; 37—*Placer Times,* July 1, 1850; 39—Downie, *Hunting for Gold,* p. 179; Yuba County Records; Parke quote, The Huntington Library; 41—Epigraph and text: Pratt quote, The Huntington Library; Yuba County Records; 42—*Sacramento Union,* February 2, 1852; Pratt quote, The Huntington Library; 43—Powers, *Tribes of California,* p. 106; Pratt quote, The Huntington Library; Swain quote, January 16, 1850, Yale University; 49—Epigraph: *North Californian,* December 5, 1857; Yuba County Records; 51—*Oroville Butte Record,* June 27, 1857; 53—Yuba County Records; 56—Adams quote, *Gold Mountain Record,* April, 1984, Yuba Feather Historical Association; 57—Butte County Court Records; 61—Epigraph: *Oroville Union Record,* June 3, 1865; *Journal of the Twelfth Session, California State Legislature,* April 15, 1861; 63—Young quote, Interview by Dorothy Hill, 1978; 64—*Oroville Union Record,* June 3, 1865; 65-69—Twogood quote, Louis E. Edwards; 71—Epigraph: May quote, Yuba Feather Historical Association; 71, 72—Twogood quote, Louis E. Edwards; 73—Merian quote, Interview by Author; 74—Caption: H. Dunning quote, Interview by Author; Twogood quote, Louis E. Edwards; 75—Hayes quote, Interview by Jann Garvis, May 17, 1987; 76—H. Dunning quote, Interview by Author; 76, 77—Twogood quote, Louis E. Edwards; 79—Epigraph: Wilkeson, *Notes on the Reconnaissance of Proposed Route of the NPRR;* 81—

McDonald and Lahore, *The Pacific Historian,* p. 26; 82—Twogood quote, Louis E. Edwards; 85—Epigraph and text: Morse quotes, Wells Fargo Bank Archives; 87—Helm quote, *Marysville Weekly Appeal,* July 14, 1882; 89—Merian quote, Interview by Author; Morse quote, Wells Fargo Bank Archives; 90—*San Francisco Examiner,* November 14, 1883; C. Falck quote, Conversation with Author, 1948; 91—Caption: C. Boles quote, E. Bowles and Bruce Levene; C. Falck quote, Conversation with Author, 1948; 92—N. Owen quote, Wells Fargo Bank Archives; 93—Collins and Levene, *Black Bart,* pp. 185, 243, 247; 95-97—Epigraph and text: Hill, *Butte Remembers,* pp. 74, 75; 103—Epigraph: J. Dunning quote, Interview by Author; 103-106—Twogood quote, Louis E. Edwards; 103—*Marysville Daily Appeal;* 104—*Butte Record,* July 5, 1904; 105—Adams quote, Sally Adams; 106—J. Dunning quote, Interview by Author, 1972; 107, 108—*Oroville Mercury,* May 9, May 27, June 11, 1910; 110-111—H. and J. Dunning quotes, Interviews by Author, 1972; 111—*Marysville Appeal Democrat,* November 19, 1915; 111-112, Terrell quote, National Archives; 115—Epigraph: Berta quote, Yuba Feather Historical Association; A. Falck quote, *Marysville Democrat,* April 26, 1923; 117—*Oroville Mercury,* September 25, October 14, 1926; 117, 118—*Oroville Mercury,* March 12, 1927; 123—Epigraph and text: *Marysville Appeal Democrat,* March 1, 1943; 125—D. Kearns quote, Conversation with Author, 1949; 126—*Splinters,* February 20, 1952; 127—E. F. Muster quote, Conversation with Author, 1960; 129—Wilhelmina Muster quote, Conversation with Author; 130—R. Brown and E. F. Muster quotes, Conversations with Author, 1966, 1972, 1968; 132—*Splinters,* September 20, 1950, February 20, 1952; *Marysville Appeal Democrat,* April 3, 1954; 133—Sundahl, *A Glimpse of Woodleaf,* Yuba Feather Historical Association; 135—Epigraph: Logan quote, Private Collection; Hadley Real Estate Company quote, Private Collection; Staff and Mitchell quote, Young Life Woodleaf; 136—C. Sundahl quote, Interview by Author, 1968; 137—Mitchell quote, Larry Entwistle and Sue Moller, Conversations with Author, 1968; 139—Staff quote, Conversation with Author, 1968; 139, 140—D. Mossinger quote, D. Mossinger; 142—Dennis Woll quote, Interview by Author, 1993; 143—Woodleaf Outdoor Education Foundation, 1994; 144—Dennis Woll, 1994.

Illustration Credits

Illustrations in this book appear through the courtesy of the following institutions, collections, and individuals, and from the following publications and documents:
Cover—Hotel, Florence Prater; Black Bart, Wells Fargo Bank; Frontispiece—Agnes Falck; Opposite 1— Smithsonian Institution; 2—left: Author's illustration after Dixon; center: *Hutchings' California Magazine,* 1860; right: Author's illustration after Dixon; 3—left: *Hutchings' California Magazine,* 1859; right: Riverside Municipal Museum; 4—Author's illustrations; 5—top: Author's illustration after Dixon; bottom: Riverside Municipal Museum; 6—Carl Mautz; 7—Author's illustrations after Dixon; 8— top: *Ballou's Pictorial Drawing Room Companion,* 1857; bottom: Author's illustration after Dixon; 9—J. R. Bartlett, *Personal Narrative of Explorations;* 10—Carl Mautz; 11— New York Public Library; 12—bottom and right: Author's illustrations; 13—Walters Art Gallery; 14—Richardson, *The Trapper's Guide;* 15—*Century Magazine;* 17—Yuba County Library, California Room; 20—Bancroft Library; 23—Browne, *A Peep at Washoe;* 24—Special Collections, Meriam Library, California State University, Chico and Siskiyou County Museum; 25—California State Library; 26—*Alta California Press,* 1850; 27—Browne, *Crusoe's Island;* 28—Private Collection; 29—*Harper's New Monthly,* 1865; 31—*Hutchings California Magazine;* 32—Ben Falck; 33—bottom: Louis E. Edwards; 34—Crocker Art Museum, Sacramento, California, E. B. Crocker Collection; 36—*Hutchings' California Magazine,* 1868; 37—*Harper's Weekly,* December 1, 1888; 38—Browne, *Crusoe's Island;* 39—The Huntington Library, San Marino, California; 40—Browne, *Indians of California;* 42—top: Yuba County Court records; bottom: Mossinger photograph; 44—Special Collections, Meriam Library, California State University, Chico and Plumas County Museum; 46—Ben Falck; 47— *Hutchings' California Magazine;* 48—Florence Prater; 50—Zelma Wood Skoog; 51—Yuba Feather Historical Association; *Harper's Weekly,* January 27, 1866; 52— Author's illustration; 53—Private Collection, Mossinger photograph; 54—top: Yuba County Court Records; bottom: Author's illustration; 55—*Harper's New Monthly Magazine,* 1860; 56—Author's illustration; 57—Denver Public Library; 58—Yuba County Court Records; 59— *Coleville's Marysville Directory,* 1855, Yuba County Library, California Room; 62, 63—Yuba Feather Historical Association; 64, 65—Louis E. Edwards; 66—Wells Fargo Bank; 67—top left: Elizabeth Merian; bottom left: *Hutchings' California Magazine;* bottom right: Author's illustration; 68—*Amy's Marysville Directory,* 1858, Yuba County Library, California Room; 69—Sandra Dunning Noel; 70—Carl Mautz; 72—Agnes Falck; 73—Thompson and West, *History of Yuba County;* 74—top: Yuba Feather Historical Association; bottom: Agnes Falck; 75—top: Yuba Feather Historical Association; 78—Private Collection;

79—Yuba Feather Historical Association; 80—top, Yuba Feather Historical Association; inset, Andrew C. Leach and Philip McDonald; 81—top: Graham and Day, *Harper's Weekly,* 1877; bottom: Yuba Feather Historical Association; 82—top: *Marysville Appeal Directory,* 1878, Yuba County Public Library, California Room; bottom: Yuba Feather Historical Association; 84-86—Wells Fargo Bank; 87— California State Library, Stellman Collection; 88—Wells Fargo Bank; 89—Calaveras County; 90—left: Wells Fargo Bank; right: Marc C. Reed Collection and Bruce Levene; 91—Earl Bowles and Bruce Levene; 92—Private Collection; 93—*Hutchings' California Magazine;* 94—Agnes Falck; 96—Ben Falck; 97—left: Lawrence Falck; right: Private Collection; 98—Sandra Dunning Noel; 99—top: Plumas County Museum, Mossinger photograph; 100— Yuba Feather Historical Association; 101—Sandra Dunning Noel; 102—Private Collection; 104—Ben Falck; 105—top: Private Collection; bottom: Sally Adams; 106— Ben Falck; 107—Ben Falck; 108—Yuba Feather Historical Association; 109—top: Sandra Dunning Noel; bottom: Ben Falck; 110—Private Collection; 111—Sandra Dunning Noel; 112—Sally Adams; 113—Yuba Feather Historical Association; 114, 116, 117—Private Collection; 118—top: Carl Mautz; bottom: Yuba Feather Historical Association; 119—Private Collection; 120—Yuba Feather Historical Association; 121—Helen Falck Dunning; 122, 124, 125, 126—Private Collection; 127—E. F. Muster; P. V. Burke; 128—E. F. Muster; 129—top: Private Collection; bottom: Irene Steinlage; 130—E. F. Muster; 131, 132—Private Collection; 133—Young Life Woodleaf; 134—Private Collection; 136, 137—Young Life Woodleaf; 138—top: DeWitt Whistler Jayne, Private Collection; bottom: Private Collection; 139, 140, 141—Private Collection; 142, 143—Educational Resource Center, Sutter County Superintendent of Schools; 144—Young Life Woodleaf; 145—Private Collection; 146—Educational Resource Center, Sutter County Superintendent of Schools.

Index